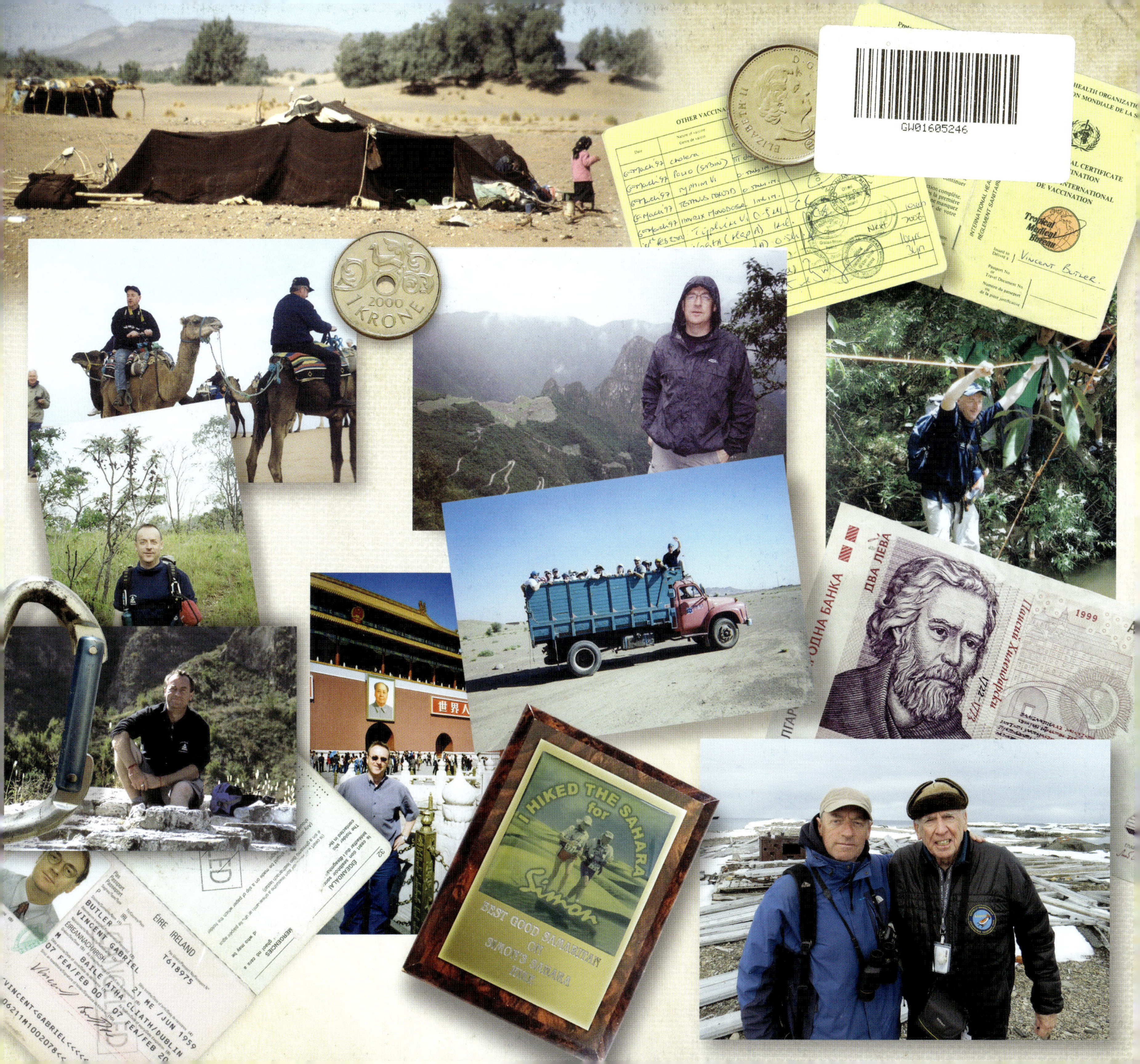
GW01605246
2000
1 KRONE
I HIKED THE SAHARA
for
Simon
ДВА ЛЕВА
1999
ÉIRE IRELAND
BUTLER
VINCENT GABRIEL
Tropical Medical Bureau

First published in 2018 by Vincent Butler

ISBN: 9781788550611

Author: Vincent Butler

Published by Vincent Butler, Newbridge, Co.Kildare
Typeset in: 10/16pt Baskerville Light
Design: Eamon Sinnott & Partners.

Front Cover Image: Glacier and icebergs, Jökulsárlón, Iceland.
Back cover image: Author and whale skeleton, Jougla Point, Antarctic Peninsula.

Sixty Photographs for Simon

Vincent Butler

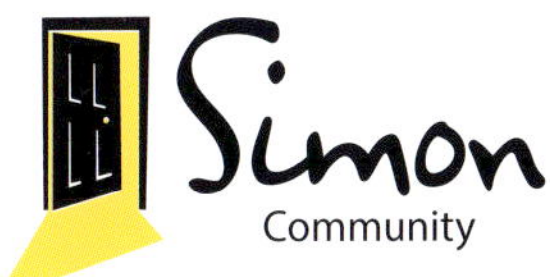

Proceeds from the sale of this book go to the Simon Community

Acknowledgements

Writing this book has been a remarkable journey and without the support of many people would never have come to fruition.

Sincere thanks to Eamon Sinnott for designing the book, Tim Severin for writing the Foreword and Conor Graham of Irish Academic Press for his advice and help in steering me through the publishing process.

For information details I am indebted to Ragnar Hauksson, Sisse Brimberg, Michael Nolan, Jim Kelley and Mark Carmody.

A special heartfelt thanks to Michelle Cooney, Archivist at the Christian Brothers Province Centre Dublin and also Br. Phil Ryan and Br. Edmund Garvey. The combined efforts of this trio culminated in my recent meeting with Br. Tom Kelly which ultimately brought my story full circle.

Special thanks to Bethan Kilfoil, Dermot Finegan, Brian Andrews, Morgan McCabe, Robbie Daly and Steven Short for their support, encouragement and advice.

I will be forever grateful to the following for their generous sponsorship and support - UCD Alumni Relations, Clinton and Missy Kelly, Mary and Noel Lee, Paddy Butler and Vivienne McBride, Sara Young and Dustin Nelson, Lindblad Expeditions, CIE Tours International, Excursions Ireland, Achill Coaches, Logans Executive Travel, Callinan Coaches, Bon Voyage Chauffeur Services, McCaffrey Coaches, Carrig Coaches, Blarney Castle - House and Gardens, Ireland With Locals, Bernard Kavanagh and Sons and Cronin's Coaches.

Many thanks for the financial support given to the project by Tony Lynch, Michael McCormack, P.G Duffy and Sons Newbridge, Noel Caffrey, John Armstrong, Killarney Jaunting Cars, The Rockshop Liscannor, Philip Byrne, Mike Banahan, Ann Ryan, Deirdre Breen, Ancestor Network, Mark Hannaford, Roy Buckley, Jim Geaney, Joan and Brendan O'Rourke, Damien Walsh, The Red Fox Inn, Kerry Coaches, Mick Moloney, Suirway Coaches, Frank Lafferty and Bartons Transport.

Much love to my wonderful wife Lindi – for everything.

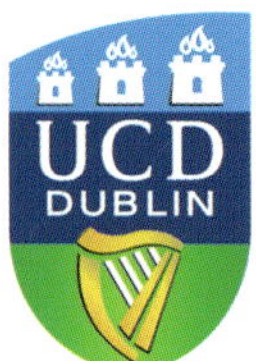

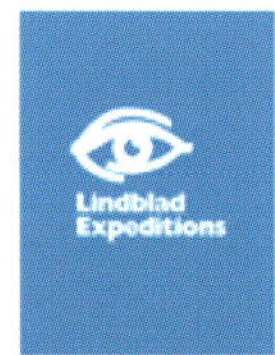

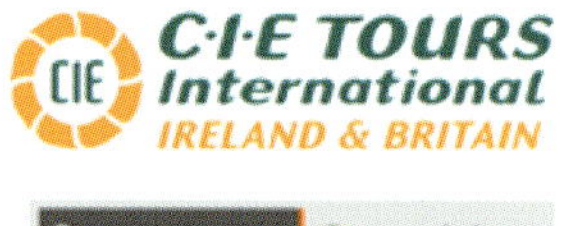

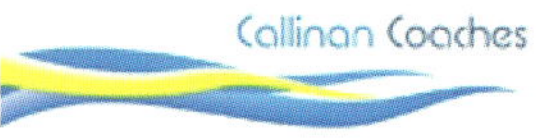

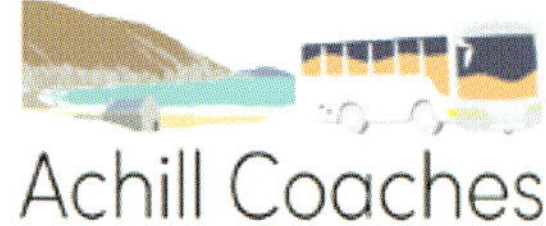

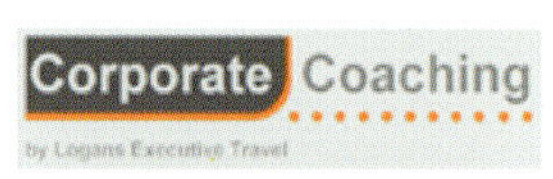

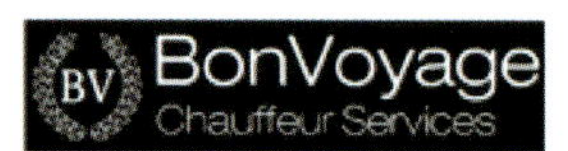

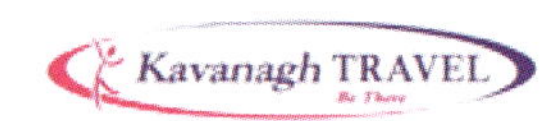

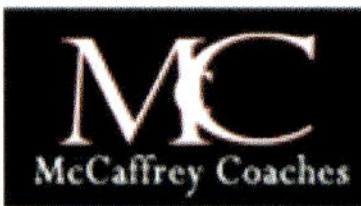

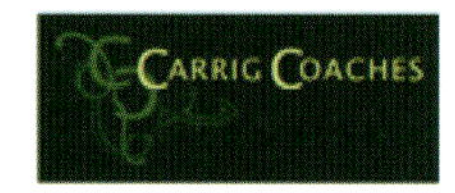

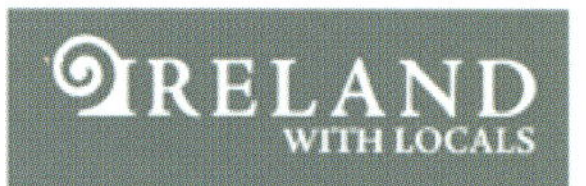

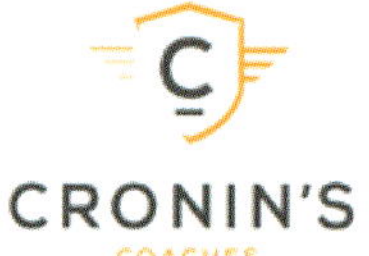

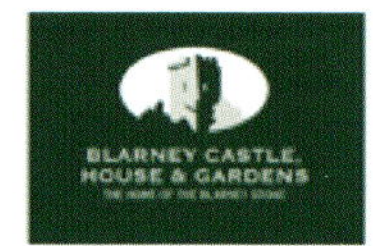

FOREWORD

Aboard the expedition ship *National Geographic Explorer* there's an evening ritual. Before they dine, the passengers take their seats in the lounge. Drinks are served. Window blinds lowered to block out the light. An array of large TV screens switched on. An air of expectation builds. Near the bar loiters the expedition's staff. Each waits his or her turn to walk to the centre of the room, step into the circular podium wryly known as the 'Circle of Truth', and speak of the day's events. An ornithologist flashes up images of birds spotted earlier that day and describes their habits. It could be a wandering albatross, or a storm petrel, or a rockhopper penguin. A geologist takes his place and talks about the rocks the passengers trudged across on their shore excursion. The botanist shows photos of wild flowers in delicate shades of pink, violet, sky blue and mauve, that he identified beside the trail. The onboard oceanographer speaks of currents, and the naturalists - there will be at least two of them - discourse on whales and dolphins, or maybe arctic foxes and walruses. Photo instructors whose day job is showing the guests how best to use their cameras, display their own pictorial record of the day.

…and then there is Vinnie. Hovering beside the bar with a gleeful expression.

Everyone in the audience looks forward to hearing Vinnie. The 'Circle of Truth' is not for him. He paces around the podium in one direction, reverses course, waves his arms, gestures at the multiple screens with the hand microphone, speaks of European Bog Bodies, or Medieval cesspits, or Holy Wells and Trees, or The Great Hunger, and Medieval butchery. And sprinkles his narrative with a bright dusting of quips and witticisms. Always in that unmistakable Dub accent.

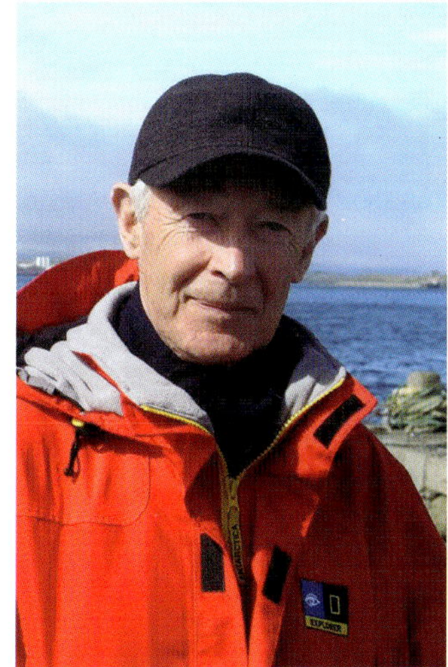

That is how I have watched Vinnie in action over this past decade … and I had no idea that he was also a secret, skilled photographer. Now he shares with us the pick of the sights he has witnessed on his travels as an itinerant historian/lecturer. Some images take me back to several of the voyages in Vinnie's company. To Faeroes and Iceland, County Galway and Scotland. Others are harvested from regions unknown to me, dramatic land- and seascapes; the homespun humanity of daily life in exotic surroundings, quirky details. Or they capture a moment: my favourite is the semi-submerged Inuit doing the 'Eskimo roll' in his kayak. It causes an involuntary shiver.

No doubt about it: Vinnie has 'the photographer's eye' – and a picture editor's sound judgement.

Vinnie's photographs are glimpses of a world, full of interest, variety and colour. It follows that we should do our best to preserve and protect its diversity. At the same time he draws attention to the fact that we can make a difference much closer to home. The proceeds of the sale of this book are to go to the Simon Community. When he asked me to write this foreword, I agreed at once. The Cork branch of Simon is my 'go to' local charity, as the Dublin branch is Vinnie's. So please support Vinnie's generosity.

I wish him and his endeavour every success.

Tim Severin

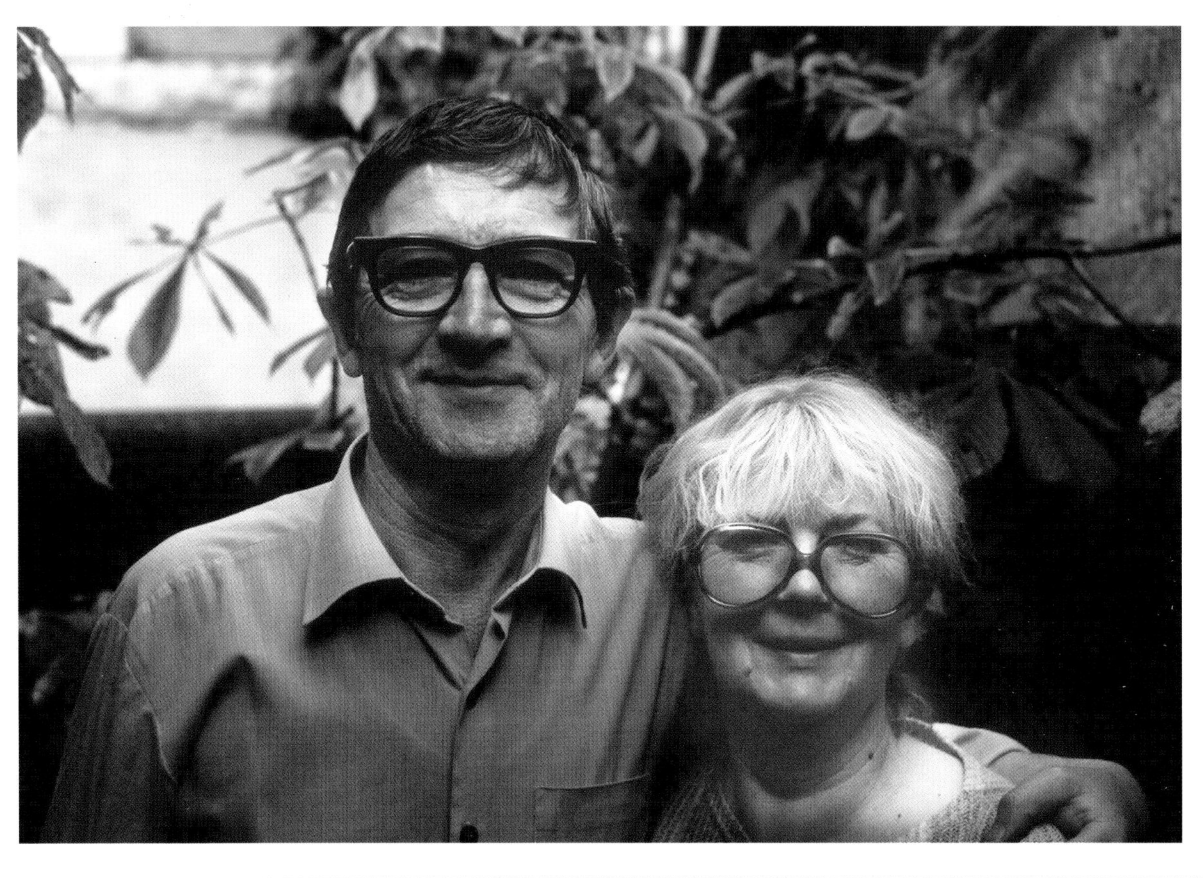

Dedicated to my wonderful parents, Patricia and Gabriel,
in loving remembrance of shared dreams.

A Big Thank You from Simon...

Imagine having no safe place to call home, not knowing where you will be living today, next week, or next month. This is the stark reality for many thousands of men, women and children in Ireland today. At the time of writing, there are nearly 10,000 people trapped in emergency accommodation and many thousands more living with housing insecurity. With the sheer scale of the crisis, it is important to remember that these numbers reflect real people and real families who are trying to live their lives in very difficult circumstances. Every person has their own story; what is common to all is that homelessness and housing insecurity is traumatic,stressful and filled with uncertainty.

We in the Simon Communities are doing everything we can in the face of this crisis, as we have been doing for almost 50 years providing much needed services and housing for thousands of people experiencing homelessness. Our key focus is working with people to address their immediate issues whilst also supporting them to plan for their future. We also have a long history of campaigning to ensure the State recognises the injustice of homelessness and responds with effective policies, services and appropriate legislation.

Access to secure, affordable housing is a major challenge but we must also provide people with supports to help address their other needs so that they can leave homelessness behind for good. Preventing homelessness and keeping people in the homes they have is critical. The huge public concern about the issues of homelessness and housing is clear to us every single day in our work in the Simon Communities; the support we receive is both inspiring and humbling. We would sincerely like to thank Vincent Butler for so generously donating the proceeds of his book, *Sixty Photographs for Simon,* to the Simon Communities and to thank all those who have supported us through purchasing it. Standing together we can make a real difference. With your continued support, our door will always be open, for as long as people need us.

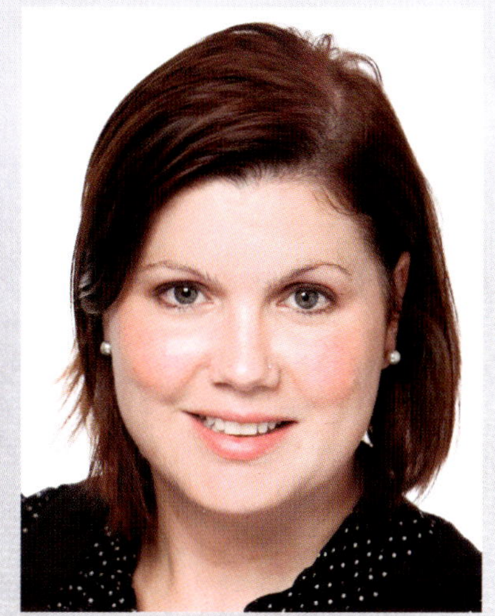

Niamh Randall,
National Spokesperson

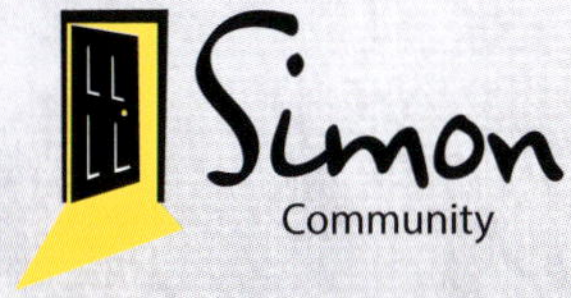

SIXTY PHOTOGRAPHS FOR SIMON INTRODUCTION

It all began in a bus shelter on the Ranelagh Road in Dublin. It was the sunny afternoon of Thursday 19th August 1999. A large, brightly coloured poster caught my eye and I paused to investigate. Dublin Simon Community were organising a trek in the Sahara to help raise funds.

To participate, a designated amount of cash had to be raised. I noted the relevant number and the next day phoned to get more details. The following week I dropped into their offices in Cope Street with the registration fee, was given an information pack, some Sahara Trek T-Shirts and a list of suggested ways to generate sponsorship. Fund-raising and fitness training were launched in earnest.

On a Saturday morning six months later, I stood amongst an enthusiastic, eclectic band of fellow trekkers in the Departures Hall of Dublin Airport. Effervescent in our enthusiasm, we were all proudly sporting our crisp, brand-new Sahara Trek T-Shirts. Clutching our boarding passes we edged slowly forward toward the security gates. The point of no return had been reached. Following months of preparation our adventure had finally begun - we were on our way at last to the shifting sands of the Sahara.

Three days later at noon I was sitting on the parched ground of a wadi in blistering heat deshelling a hard-boiled egg. I was salmon pink, foot-blistered, unshaven, uncombed and dust-speckled. By now my brand-new Sahara Trek T-Shirt was far from being crisp. During the morning we had traversed a high ridge and then trekked eight miles across a series of low dunes and were now enjoying a well-earned light lunch. The landscape was stunningly beautiful. I was mesmerised by it all. There was a heart-warming camaraderie. The day before, we had been arranged into manageable groups of twenty or so. Each was led from the front by a local guide, with a second one, who worked for Across the Divide, covering the back. This English-based company had organised the trek and was overseeing its day-to-day logistics. Thus safely sandwiched, we perambulated along our route.

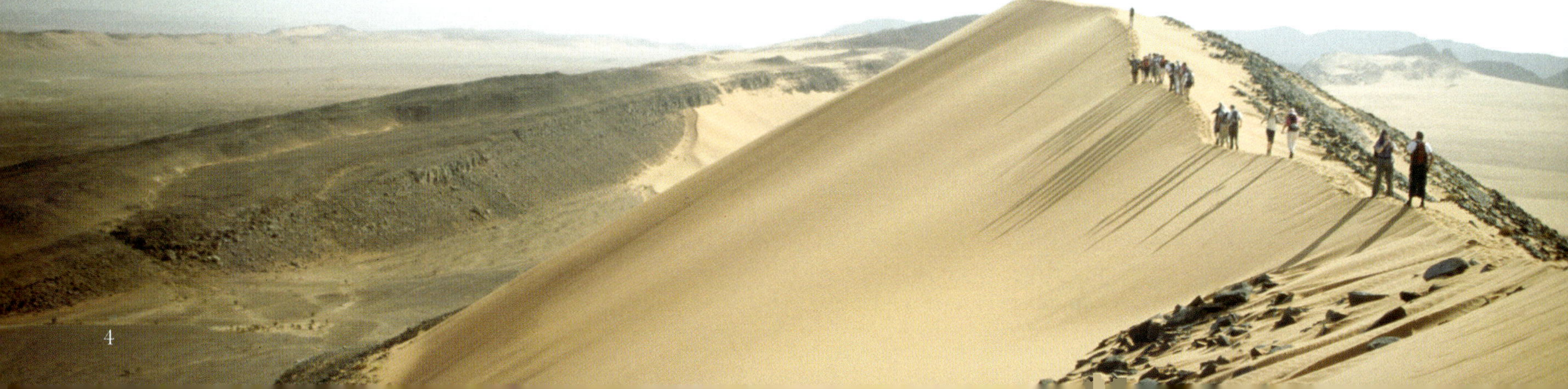

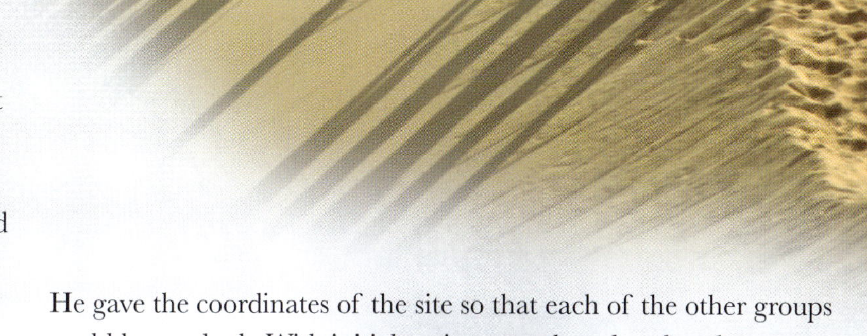

I was in the lead group that afternoon, the first to quit lunch and head off into the shimmering heat, trail blazers for the other five or six groups who would follow on.

Around mid-afternoon we were making our way across a plain. It seemed to stretch into infinity, to be edgeless. As an avid collector, with a lifelong interest in geology and a professional background in archaeology, I was in seventh heaven. The ground was festooned with angular boulders, cobbles and sand, all by-products of the continual cycle of diurnal temperature changes. I was toward the back of the group eagerly scanning the ground for rock samples that I could use as teaching props. A piece of porcelain-like stone caught my eye. I stopped, picked it up and stared at it wide-eyed. I was holding a fragment of a small flint projectile that had been fashioned by human hands. I flicked it over, examining its every feature. A sweeping scan of the ground revealed a wide scatter of additional flakes. I picked up several.

Beyond doubt, we had just walked onto the remains of a prehistoric site known as a knapping-floor, where flint had been worked to produce tools and weapons. I shouted to the others in our group to stop and when they had gathered around, explained the significance of the discovery. There was a wave of excitement. Dan, our Across the Divide guide radioed back to Mark, the expedition leader, and a director of that company, to tell him about the find.

He gave the coordinates of the site so that each of the other groups could have a look. With initial excitement abated and under pressure for time, we continued on our way.

That evening Mark asked me if I would be willing to talk about what I had discovered during his evening briefing to the group. I was more than happy to oblige and with my fellow trekkers ensconced around a blazing camp fire I expounded on the nature of the find and things archaeological. We had been informed that the following day we would skirt around the edge of a mountain, the rocks of which were rich in fossils. Since my boyhood I have had a keen interest in palaeontology so I was understandably excited when Mark inquired if I had any knowledge of fossils, and if so, would I be willing to go out in the lead group in the morning, position myself at a designated place with a staff radio and explain about the geological wonders of the spot to each group as they arrived. I leapt at the chance and it all went swimmingly well. I swapped contact details with Mark at Ouarzazate Airport at the end of the trek and returned home with 52 used rolls of slide film and an extremely heavy haversack.

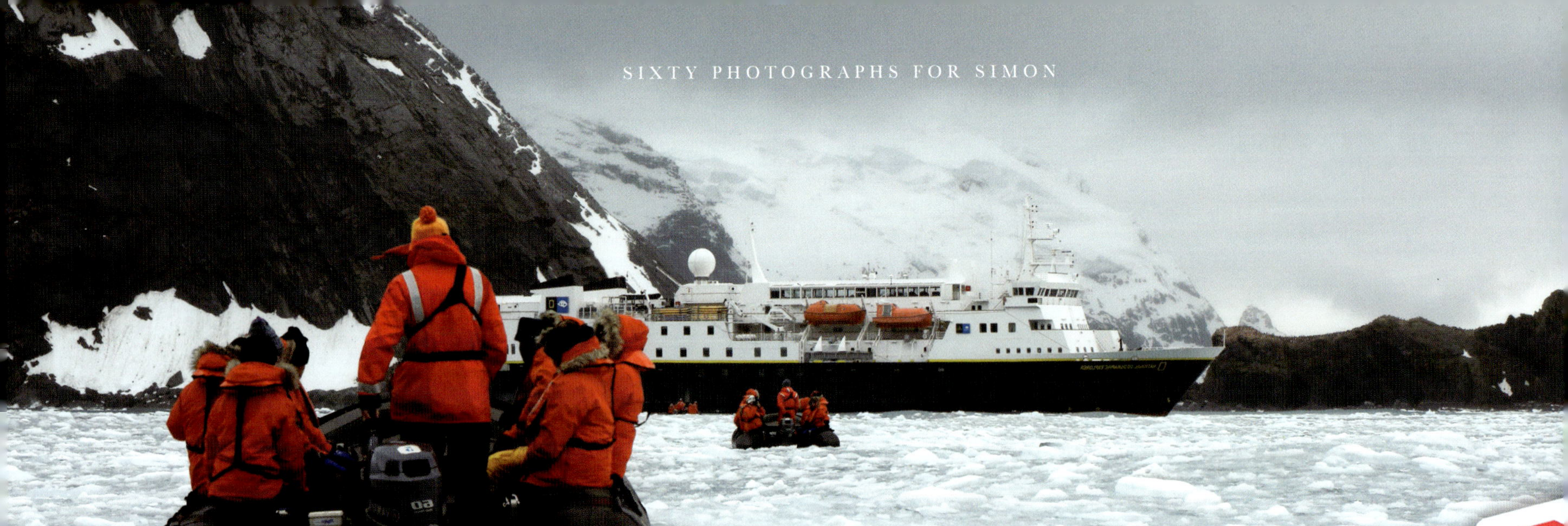

Back then I ran a small business providing educational fieldtrips for primary and secondary school students based on their history and geography curricula. While I was doing well enough, there was a definite need to find additional work to fill gaps in my workload and to keep the proverbial wolf at bay. The coffers were somewhat low that year as the summer spent itself and there was not an encouraging number of confirmed tour bookings on my business calendar.

The call that was to change everything came out of the blue in mid-August, five months after I had returned from the Sahara. It was Mark on a satellite phone in the Namibian Desert. He had been contacted by an American company called Lindblad Expeditions whom he had worked for. They were looking for someone to lead a small group on a land-based tour of Morocco for two weeks that coming November. He had recommended me for the job and wanted to check to see if I would be interested.

Right: National Geographic Explorer
Far Right: Vincent addressing fellow passengers from the 'Circle of Truth' onboard the National Geographic Explorer.

The following year Lindblad Expeditions contracted me as a lecturer working on their cruise ships and Mark signed me up as an expedition leader in his trekking company.

As a Christmas present last year, my darling wife Lindi gave me a most engaging book which charts and details the history of travel. An informative and highly illustrated tome, it was the catalyst which sparked the embryonic concept that was to develop into the present volume. Like a Saharan sand dune which grows grain by grain, so *Sixty Photographs For Simon* formed image by image and word by word.

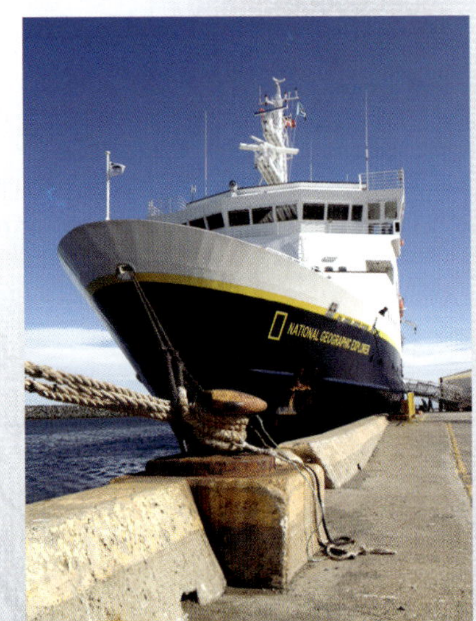

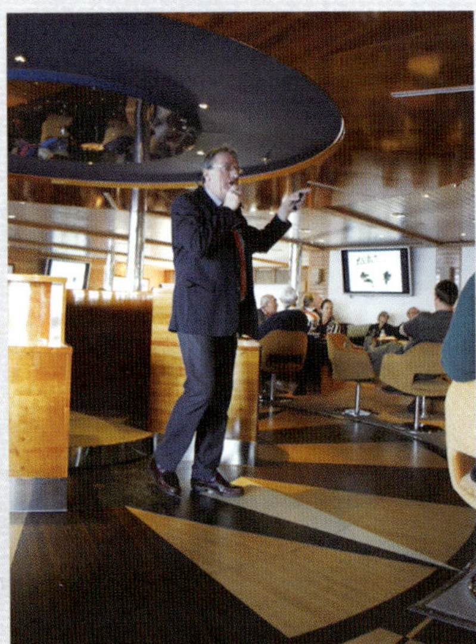

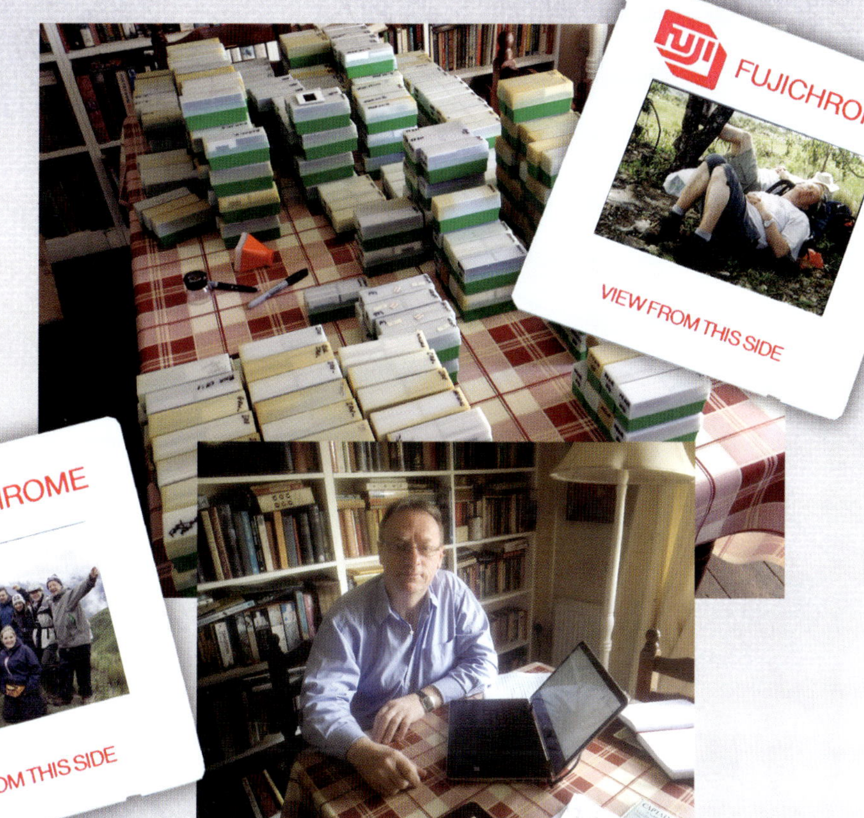

Compiling this book has been an extraordinary journey in its own right. From start to finish along the uncharted route, the support, advice and encouragement given to me by my wife Lindi and copious numbers of friends and colleagues has been second to none. All integral to the narrative, it has been wonderful to recall so many of the local people, fellow travellers, staff and friends with whom I shared so many remarkable experiences and adventures. I have myriads of treasured memories.

Little had I realised, as I strolled away from that scatter of ancient flints, how that pure chance find would ultimately open up the World to me, a life-changing moment for sure.

For some time now I have wanted to give something back. *Sixty Photographs For Simon* is that something. Heartfelt thanks to you the reader for purchasing the book, and in so doing, supporting the Simon Community in its Trojan work with the homeless.

Vincent Butler

The trek in 2000 was just over sixty miles long and this logistical detail is honoured in the title. Symbolically each image represents a mile along that wonderous, circuitous route through the desert. Subscribing to the axiom 'dreams don't work unless you do' I began the initial groundwork for the project at the beginning of January this year. Selecting the photographs was in retrospect the most arduous task of the entire project. For four full weeks I slowly trawled through my archive of 22,000 digital images and 35 mm slides arrayed in serried ranks of boxes and folders on our dining room table. During this process a large number of 'potentials' were initially chosen from which a seemingly unending number of lists were drafted and redrafted as numerous images were revisited, reconsidered and replaced. So it was with an immense sense of relief that I finally transferred the sixty 'finalists' to their designated folder. The photographs were now in place so I began work on the words.

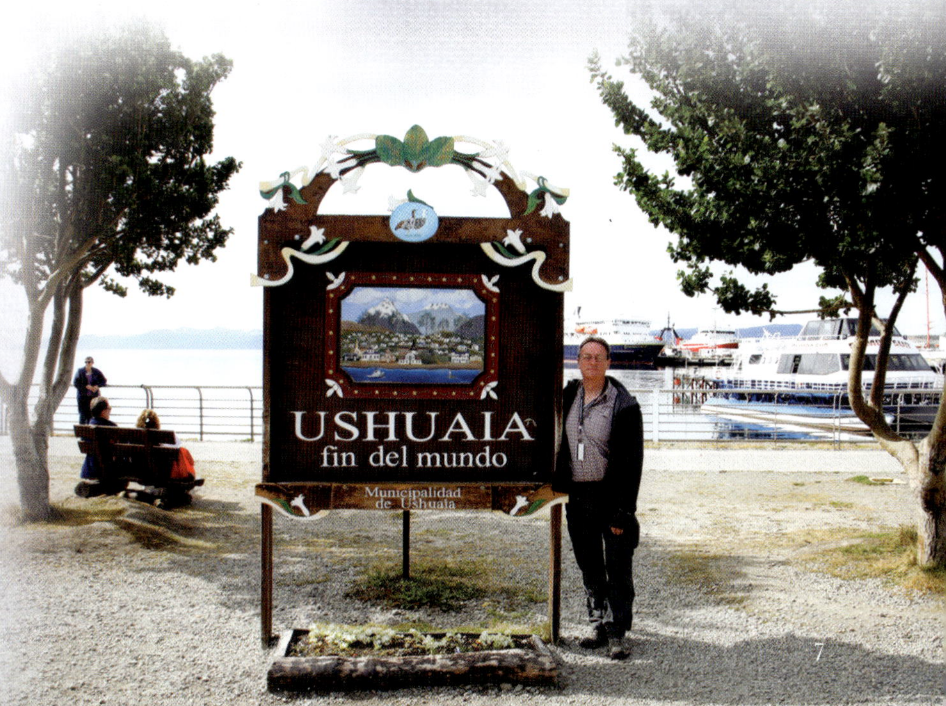

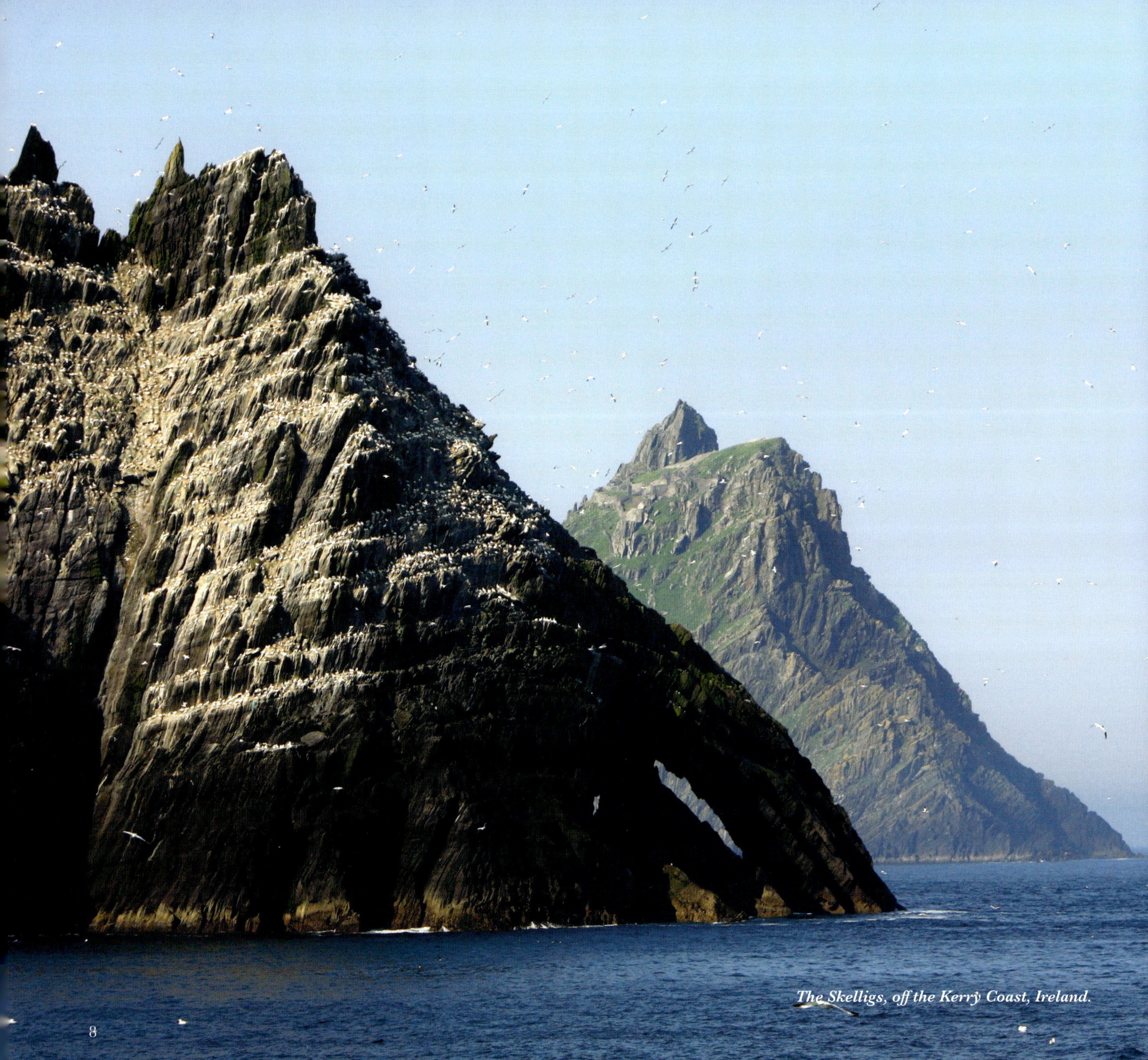

The Skelligs, off the Kerry Coast, Ireland.

ABOUT THE AUTHOR

Boyhood interests in natural history, archaeology and geology were later to be the foundation blocks for a career focused on imparting knowledge. Vincent graduated from UCD in 1981 with an MA degree and subsequently worked for a number of years as an osteoarchaeologist in the National Museum of Ireland.

A freelance heritage specialist, he designs and delivers educational programmes and lectures on a wide spectrum of subjects both at home and abroad. In the varied guises of expedition leader, guide and tour director he has travelled widely over the last 20 years. Involved in Irish tourism since the early 1990s, Vincent is one of Ireland's leading tour guide trainers.

A keen photographer, he is extremely fortunate to be able to visit remote areas in the world aboard the expedition cruise ship, the *National Geographic Explorer,* where he works as a senior lecturer. This platform has allowed him to develop his skills in landscape, wildlife and cultural photography.

Vincent lives in Newbridge with his wife Lindi and their two stuffed pheasants, Willow and Zulu.

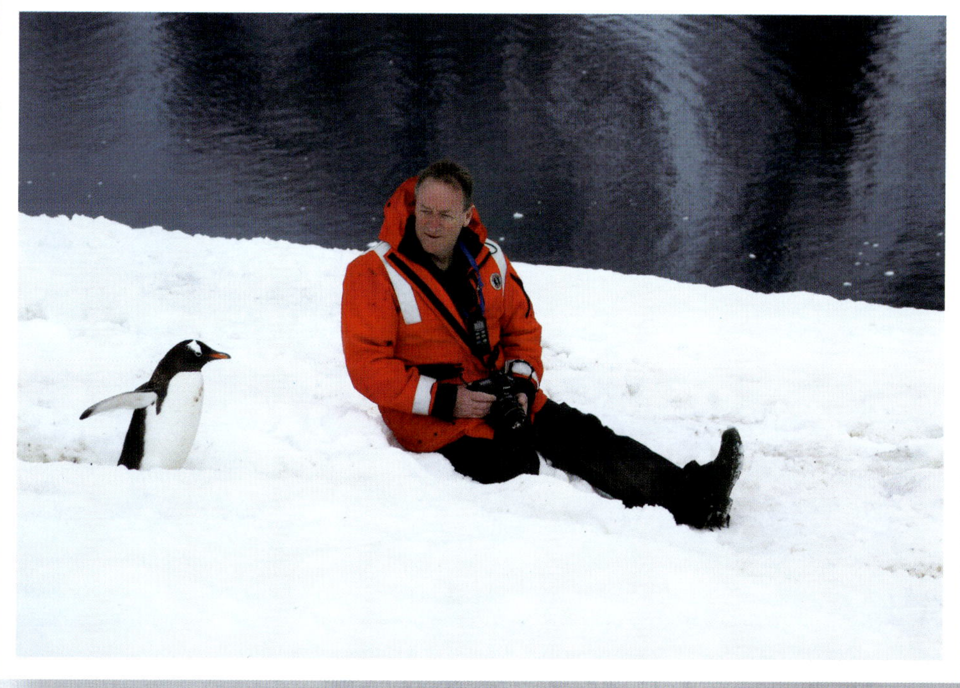

Charting our Journey...

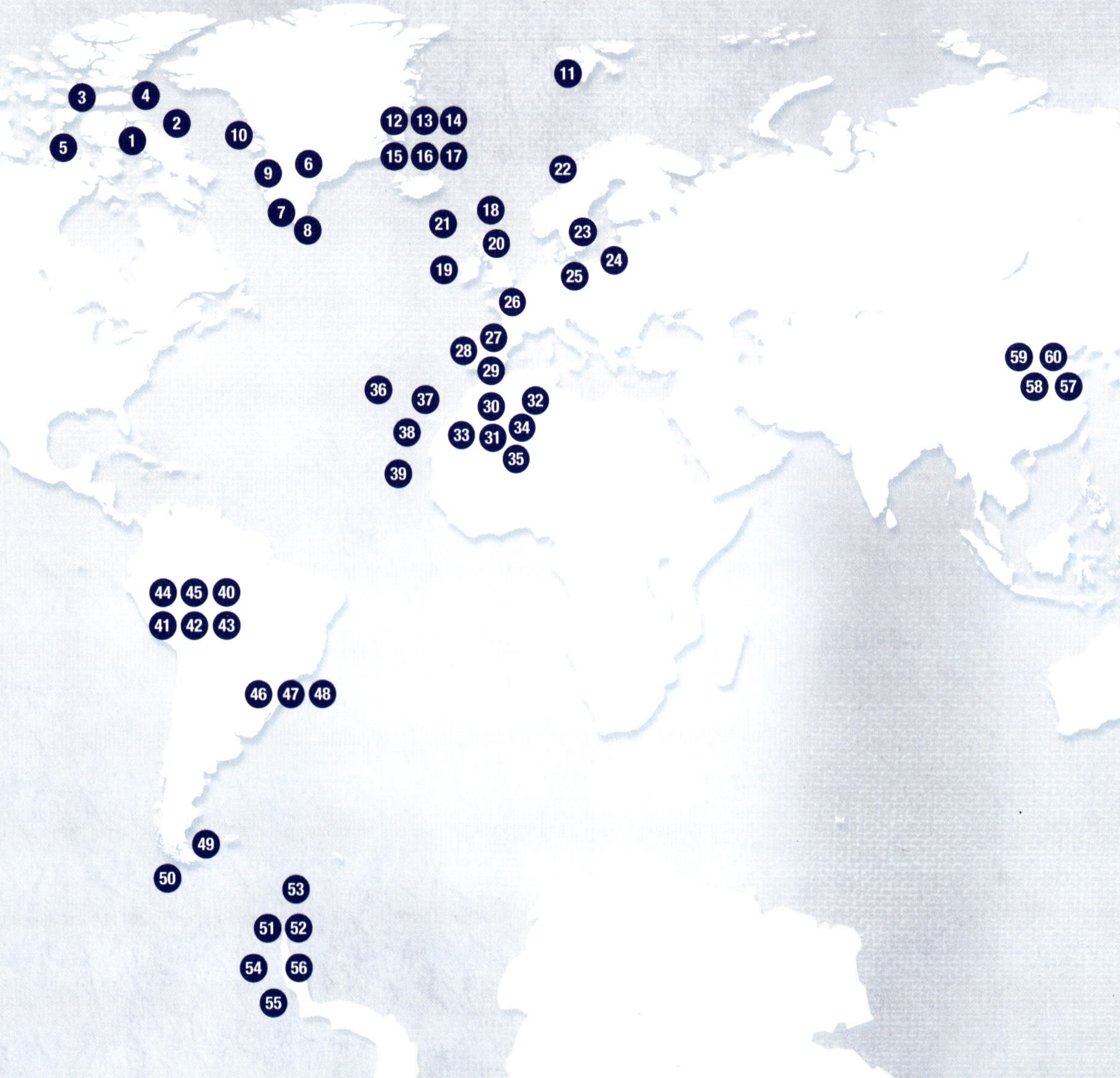

IMAGE SEQUENCE AND GENERAL DETAIL

Image 1 Icebergs, Pond Inlet, Baffin Island, Canadian Arctic
Image 2 Male Polar Bear, Hoare Bay, Baffin Island, Canadian Arctic
Image 3 Franklin Expedition Graves, Beechey Island, Canadian Arctic
Image 4 'Sunset', Baffin Bay, Canadian Arctic
Image 5 CCGS Pierre Radisson, Franklin Strait, Canadian Arctic
Image 6 A Day's Catch, Qaqortoq, Greenland
Image 7 Tidewater Glacier, Prins Christian Sund, Greenland
Image 8 Fin Whale, Greenland
Image 9 Kayak Roll, Nuuk, Greenland
Image 10 Iceberg Arch, Greenland
Image 11 Walrus, Hamburgbukta, Spitsbergen, Svalbard
Image 12 Pompeii of the North, Heimaey, Westmann Islands, Iceland
Image 13 Puffins, Vigur Island, Isafjord, Iceland
Image 14 Tectonic Plates, Grjótagjá, Iceland
Image 15 Male Killer Whale, Westmann Islands, Iceland
Image 16 Icelandic Horse, Hveragerdi, Iceland
Image 17 Surtsey, Westmann Islands, Iceland
Image 18 Kvivik, Streymoy, Faeroes
Image 19 Lazy Beds, Killary Harbour, Galway, Ireland
Image 20 Lindi and Gunnera, Inverewe Gardens, Scotland
Image 21 Cleits, Hirta, St.Kilda, Outer Hebrides, Scotland
Image 22 Processing Cod, Reine, Lofoten Islands, Norway
Image 23 Rock Carvings, Grebbestad, Tanum, Sweden
Image 24 Floral Tribute, Auschwitz II-Birkenau, Poland
Image 25 Medieval Dog Paw Prints, Lubeck, Germany
Image 26 British Commonwealth Cemetery, Bayeux, France
Image 27 Resting Pilgrims, Santiago de Compostella, Spain
Image 28 Snail Seller, Lisbon, Portugal
Image 29 Macaque Monkeys, Gibraltar
Image 30 Tannery, Fez, Morocco
Image 31 'Self-Trim', Berber Market, Amizmiz, Atlas Mountains, Morocco
Image 32 Fossil Sea-Lilies, Erfoud, Morocco
Image 33 Djemma el Fna, Marrakesh, Morocco
Image 34 Saharan Sand Dunes, Oued Mbidia, Morocco
Image 35 Berber Nomads, Bouziane, Morocco
Image 36 Gorreana Tea Plantation, Sao Miguel, Azores, Portugal
Image 37 Black Scabbard Fish, Funchal, Madeira, Portugal
Image 38 Striped Dolphin and Remora, La Gomera, Canary Islands, Spain
Image 39 Pico do Fogo, Fogo Island, Cape Verde Islands
Image 40 Souvenir Seller, Ollantaytambo, Peru
Image 41 Traditional Andean Home, Angascocha, Peru
Image 42 Ancestor Shrine, Ollantaytambo, Peru
Image 43 Ploughing with Oxen, Soqma, Peru
Image 44 Machu Picchu, Peru
Image 45 Potato Celebration, Cachicata, Peru
Image 46 Chapada dos Veadeiros National Park, Goiás, Brazil
Image 47 Crystal Seller, Alto Paraíso de Goiás, Brazil
Image 48 'The World At His Feet', Sao Jorge, Brazil
Image 49 Ushuaia, Tierra del Fuego, Argentina
Image 50 Sei Whale 'Footprint' and Black- Browed Albatross, Beagle Channel, Tierra del Fuego, Argentina
Image 51 Landscape Panorama, Gerlache Strait, Antarctic Peninsula
Image 52 Adélie Penguin, Brown Bluff, Antarctic Peninsula
Image 53 Point Wild, Elephant Island, Antarctica
Image 54 Gentoo Penguin with Chicks, Jougla Point, Antarctic Peninsula
Image 55 Leopard Seal, Cierva Cove, Antarctic Peninsula
Image 56 Gentoo Penguins, Danco Island, Antarctic Peninsula
Image 57 Goat Herder, Xinchen, China
Image 58 Processing Maize, Hua Lou Gou, China
Image 59 Inquisitive Pig, Ganfang, China
Image 60 The Great Wall, Jinshanling, China

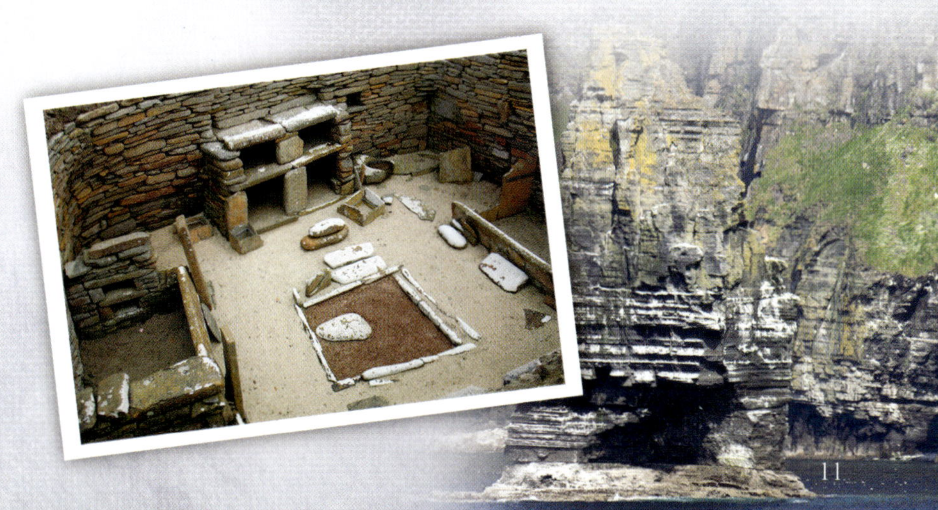

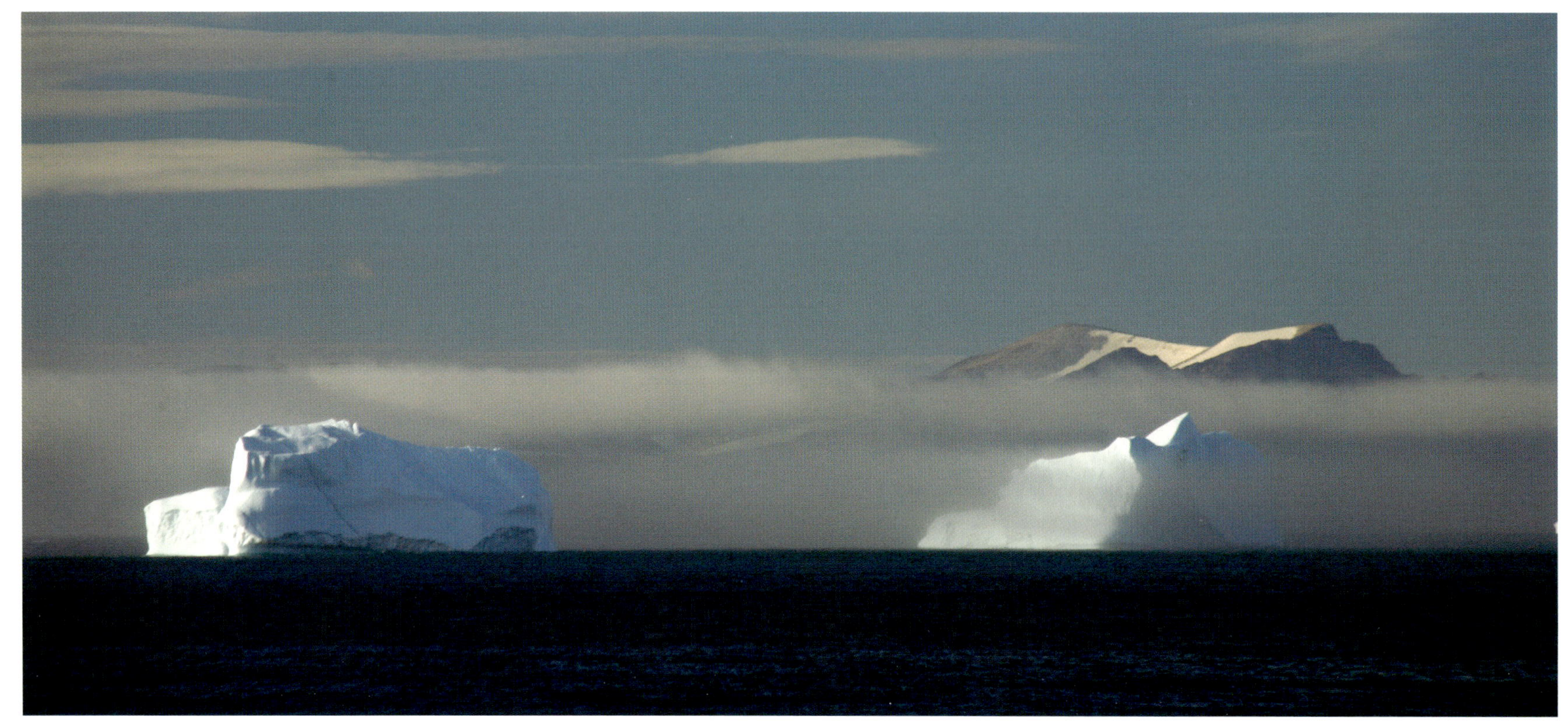

1. ICEBERGS, POND INLET, BAFFIN ISLAND, CANADIAN ARCTIC

The light breaking through early morning mist highlights two drifting icebergs. When the snout of a glacier reaches the sea large pieces break off the ice front. This process is called calving and it can be a very spectacular event. The icebergs float because ice is less dense than seawater and are carried along on ocean currents. The bulk of an iceberg, around 85–90%, lies below the surface.

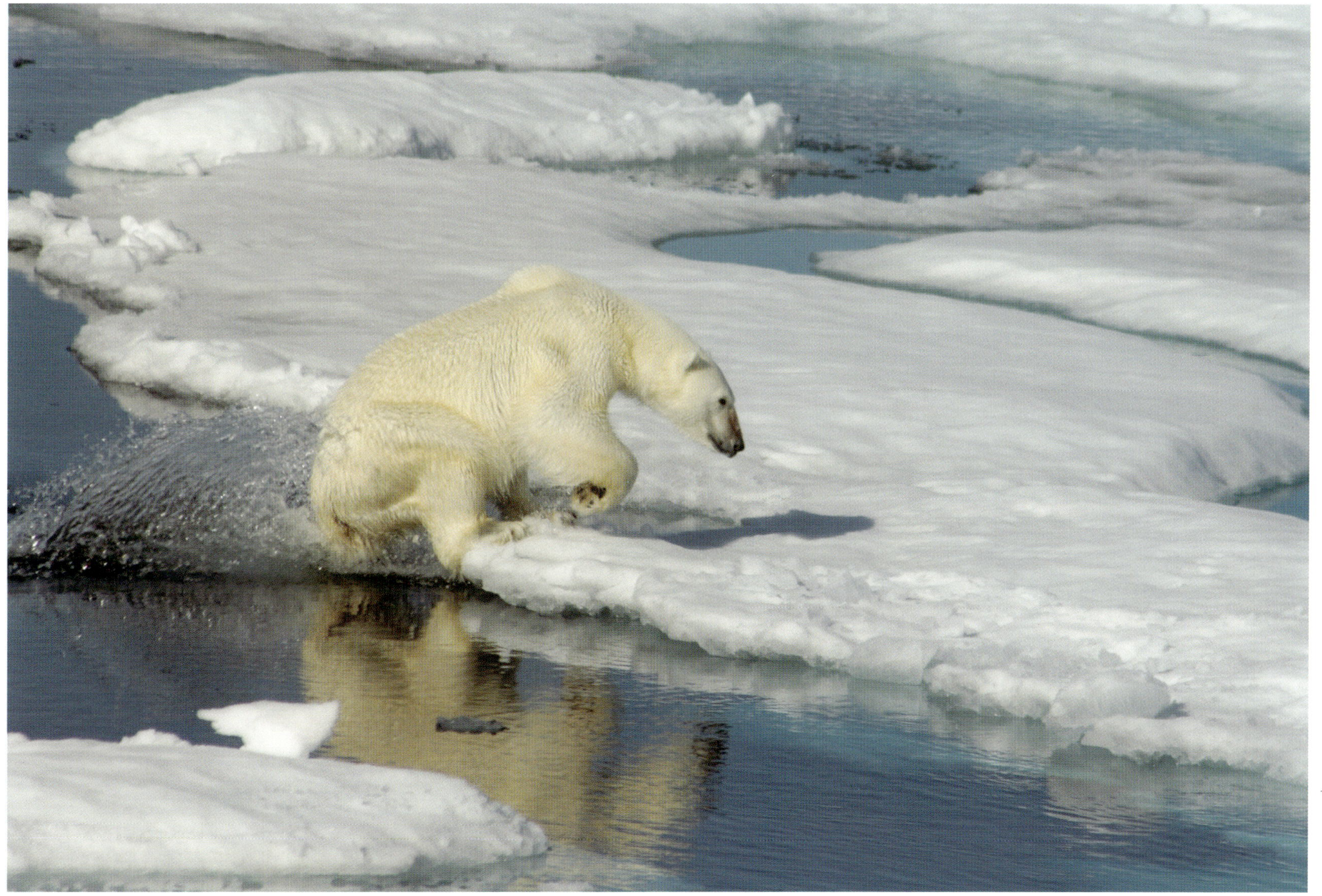

2. Male Polar Bear, Hoare Bay, Baffin Island, Canadian Arctic

A male polar bear slightly misgauges the gap while leaping between two ice floes. The largest species of bear in the world, a male can weigh as much as 128 stone and reach in excess of 10 feet when standing upright. Females are around a third of the weight of a large male. The off-white fur helps them to blend in with their surroundings, a great advantage for this top predator. With a powerful physique and partially webbed front feet, they are capable swimmers. Ringed seals are the main prey which they hunt out on the sea ice.

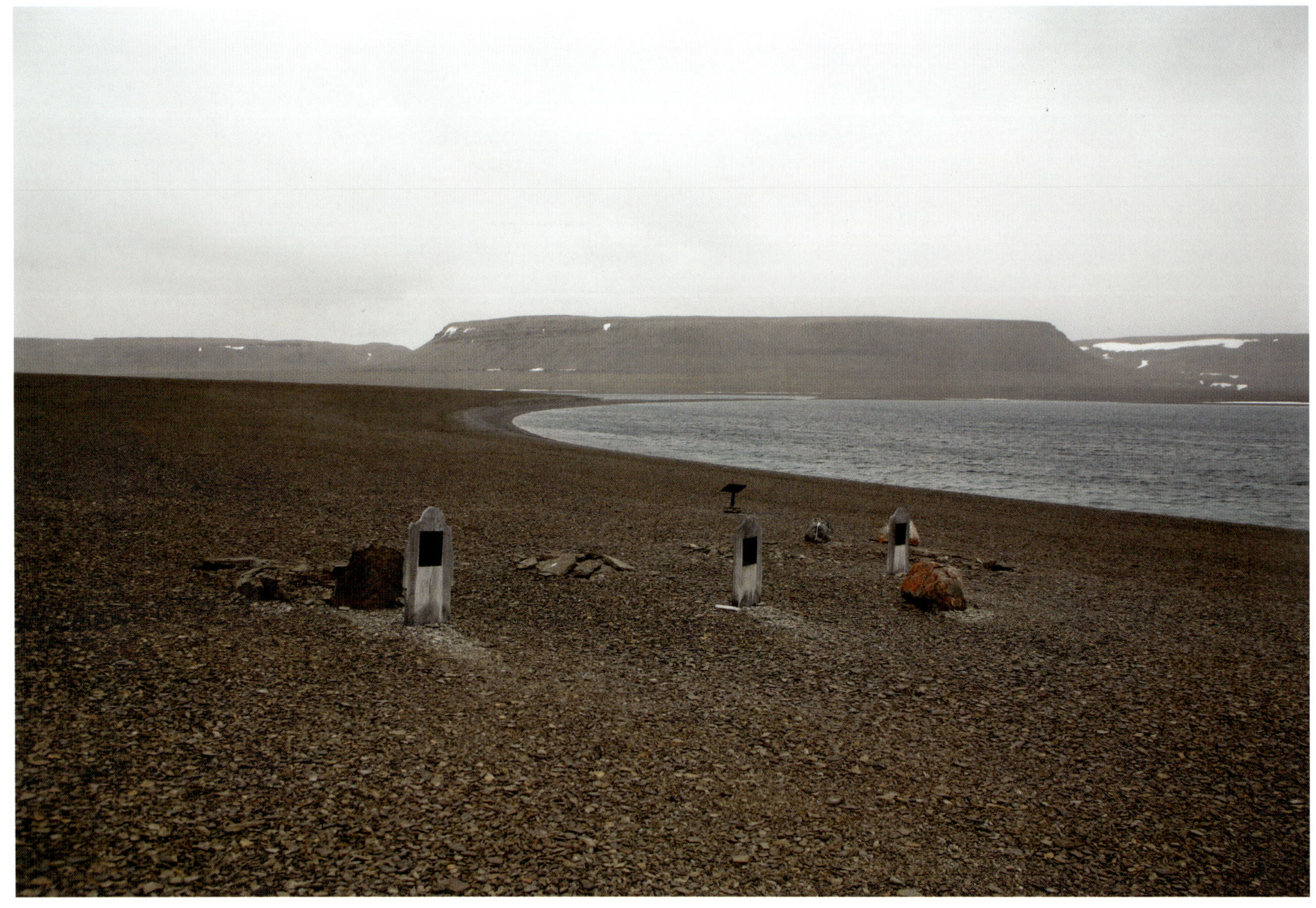

3. Franklin Expedition Graves, Beechey Island, Canadian Arctic

Three weathered grave-markers stand on a gravel terrace on desolate Beechey Island. They mark the resting place of crewmen from the Franklin Expedition. In May 1845 Sir John Franklin, with two ships, the *Erebus* and *Terror*, and 128 officers and seamen, embarked on what was then the best equipped and largest expedition ever mounted by the British in the quest for the long sought after Northwest Passage. Having overwintered at Beechey, the ships sailed towards the west when spring arrived in 1846. A high price was to be paid for their efforts to chart the elusive passage. Franklin and his entire crew perished amid the frozen wastes of the maze-like archipelago of the Canadian Arctic. May this trio, and all of their lost comrades whose remains lie scattered across the Arctic tundra, rest at ease in their celestial hammocks.

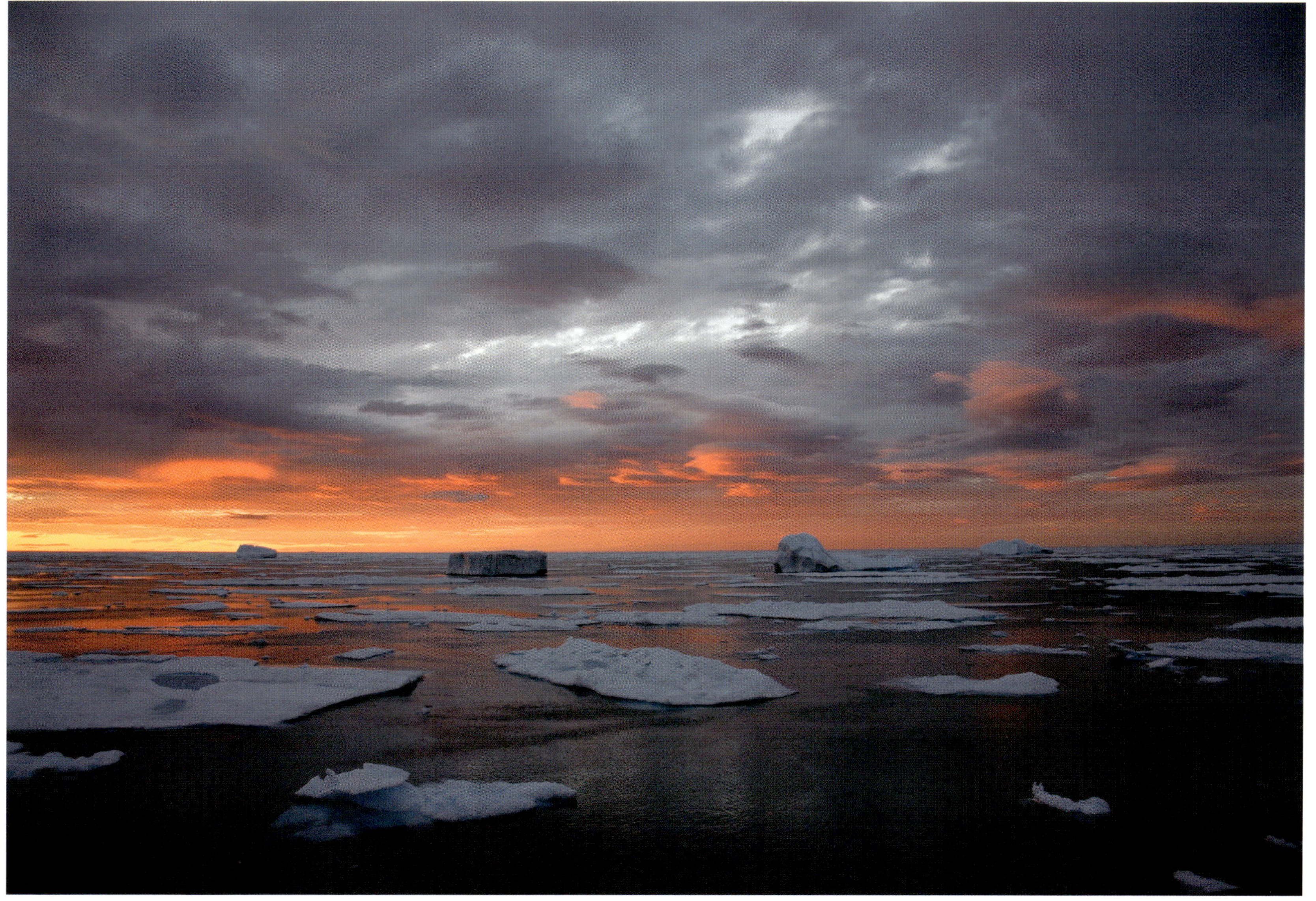

4. 'SUNSET', BAFFIN BAY, CANADIAN ARCTIC

The Arctic landscape is stunningly beautiful. The silence is almost palpable, the scale breathtaking. A complex and delicately balanced ecosystem has evolved over a lengthy sweep of time. Millennia ago small bands of people were drawn to this place of ice in search of food. Adept hunters, they developed sophisticated technologies and equipment to adapt to, and ultimately survive and flourish in, one of the harshest and most unforgiving environments on the planet. They gazed as we do today on the same wide sea vistas of drift ice, icebergs and sky set ablaze by 'sunsets' and undoubtedly pondered, just like us, on the wonder and marvel of it all.

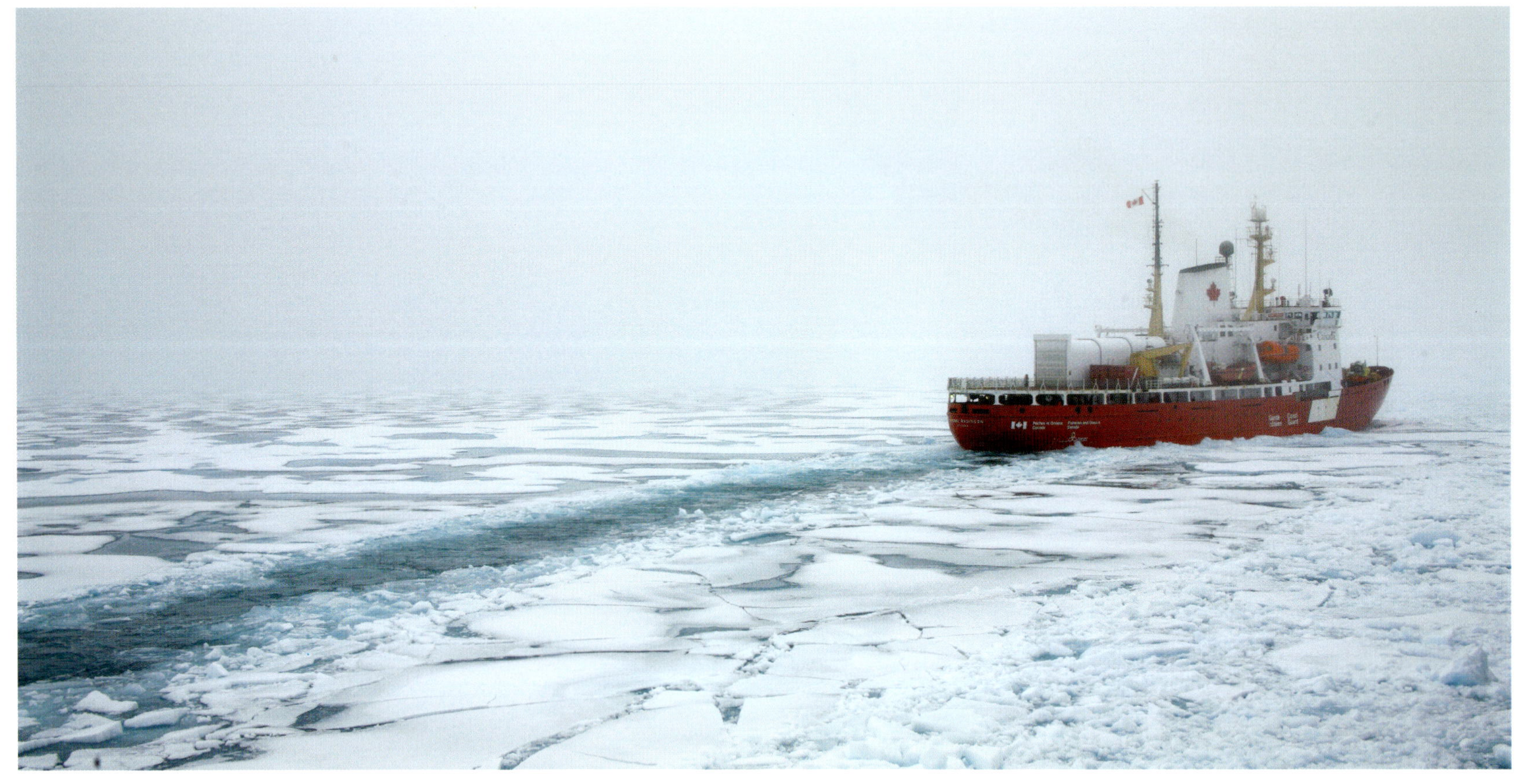

5. CCGS Pierre Radisson, Franklin Strait, Canadian Arctic

The 13,000 horsepower *CCGS Pierre Radisson* endeavors, with powerful downward thrusts of its reinforced bow, to open a passage in the ice-choked waters of Franklin Strait through which the *National Geographic Explorer* might follow. Isolated communities in the Canadian Arctic are very much dependent on the delivery of goods by ship. Icebreakers are needed to help keep waterways open to facilitate shipping activities. The Canadian Government employs the services of a number of vessels to do this and also works closely with the growing numbers of expedition cruise ships which visit the area during the summer months.

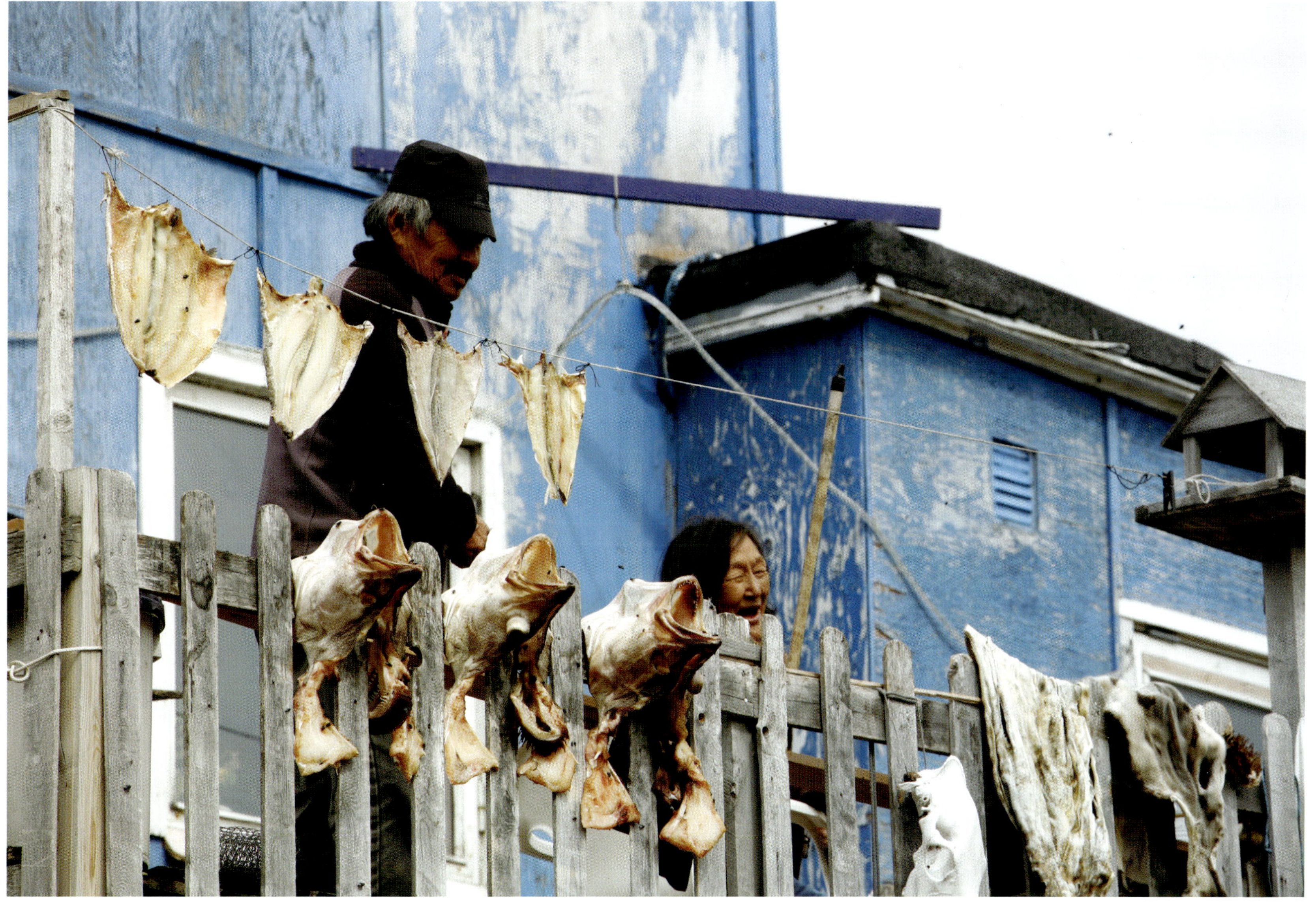

6. A DAY'S CATCH, QAQORTOQ, GREENLAND

Qaqortoq is the largest town in South Greenland. Founded in the late 18th century as a trading base it has a population of around 3,000. Commercial fishing, sea transport and a growing tourism sector are main employers. Age-old techniques are still used by the locals to catch fish for themselves. Small batches of cod and other species in varying stages of processing are an ubiquitous sight around the town. These are attached to fences and hung up on lines to dry in the air. Seal hunting provides skins and meat. Its liver, an important source of vitamin C, is eaten raw.

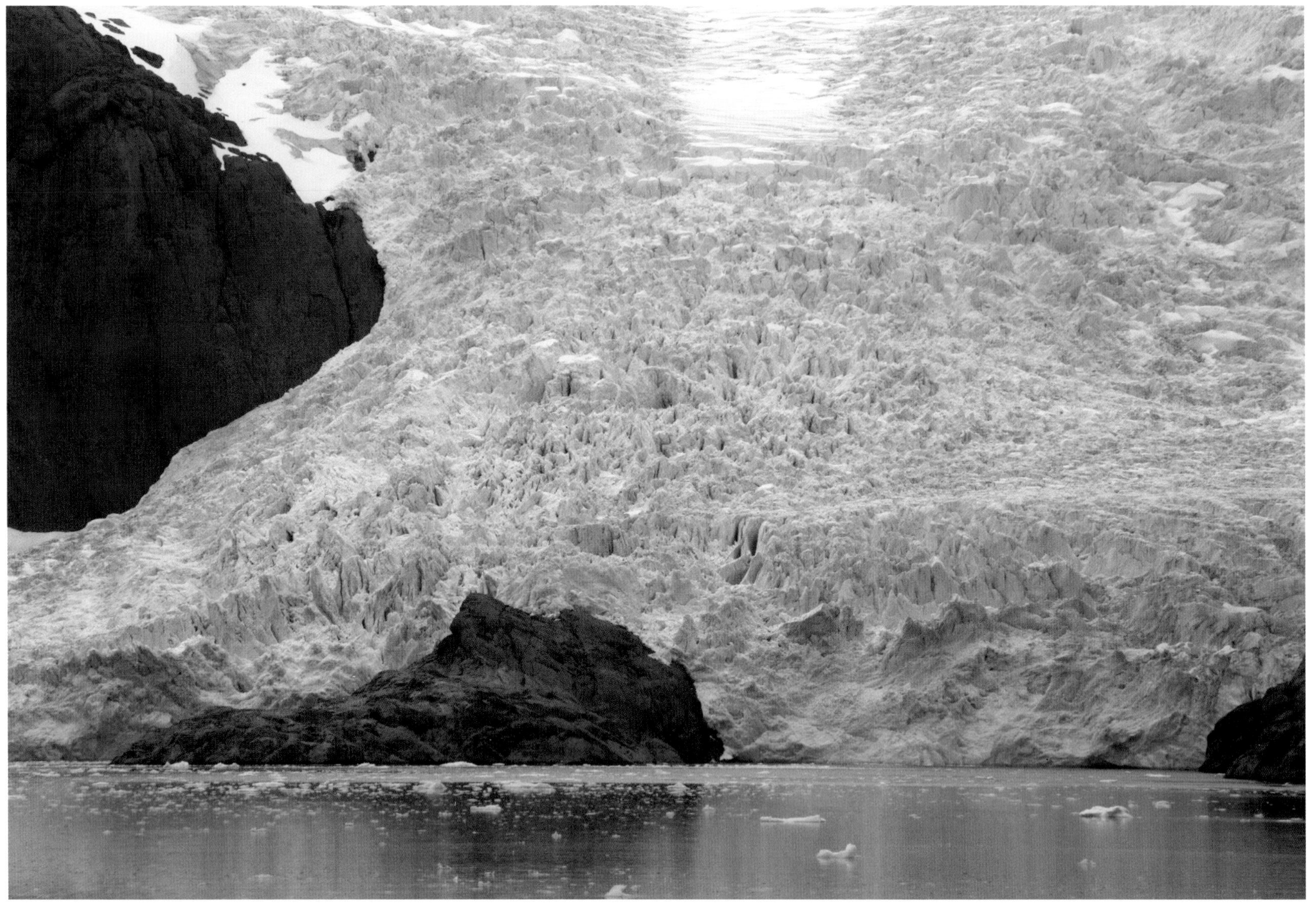

7. TIDEWATER GLACIER, PRINS CHRISTIAN SUND, GREENLAND

A valley glacier reaches the sea in a fjord on the south coast of Greenland. As it moves downslope the upper part flows somewhat faster than the lower section of the glacier which is under more pressure because of the weight of the overlying ice. This causes the ice higher up to crack, the sound of which is comparable to a cannon being fired. Gaping crevasses appear and widen as the glacier is continuously being pushed forward due to the massive pressure behind. Perhaps tens of thousands of years old, the ice formed as snow was compressed and compacted over long periods of time. When a valley glacier reaches the sea it is known as a tidewater glacier.

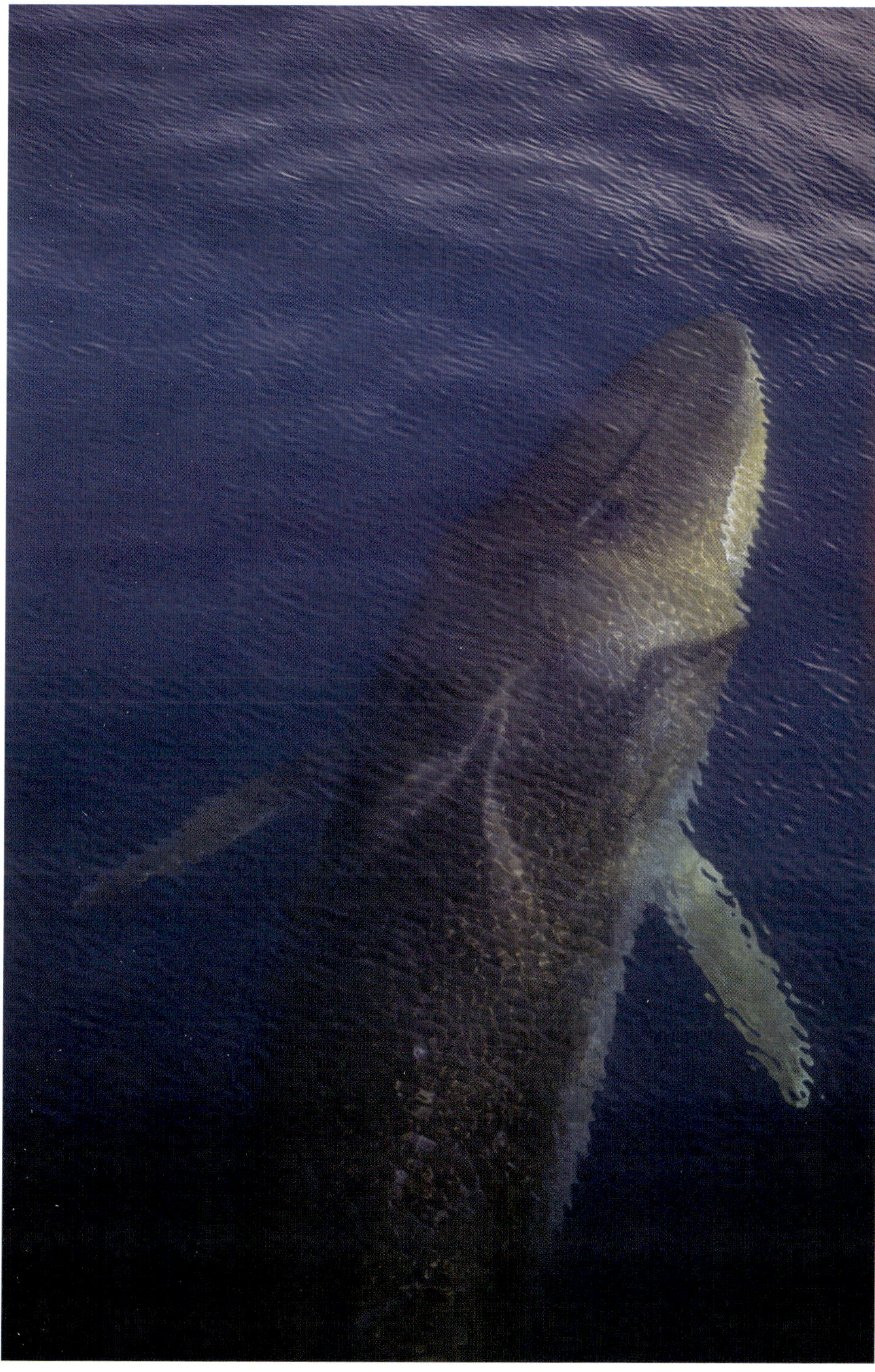

8. Fin Whale, Greenland

A fin whale glides close to the surface off the south coast of Greenland. These are the second-largest living animal on Earth after the blue whale. Adults average around 70 feet in length and can weigh up to 80 tons. Capable of swimming at speeds of up to 23 miles per hour, fin whales have acquired the nickname 'greyhound of the sea'. They are filter-feeders and have rows of overlapping plates, known as baleen, hanging vertically from the roof of the mouth. These are made from keratin and are frayed along their inner edges. When feeding the whale takes in a large quantity of water into it mouth. This is then squeezed back out through the baleen plates, the frayed inner edges of which act as a highly effective sieve. Krill and small schooling fish that have been strained from the water are then swallowed. The baleen, also known as 'whalebone' was made into stays for corsets and bodices in the 19th century.

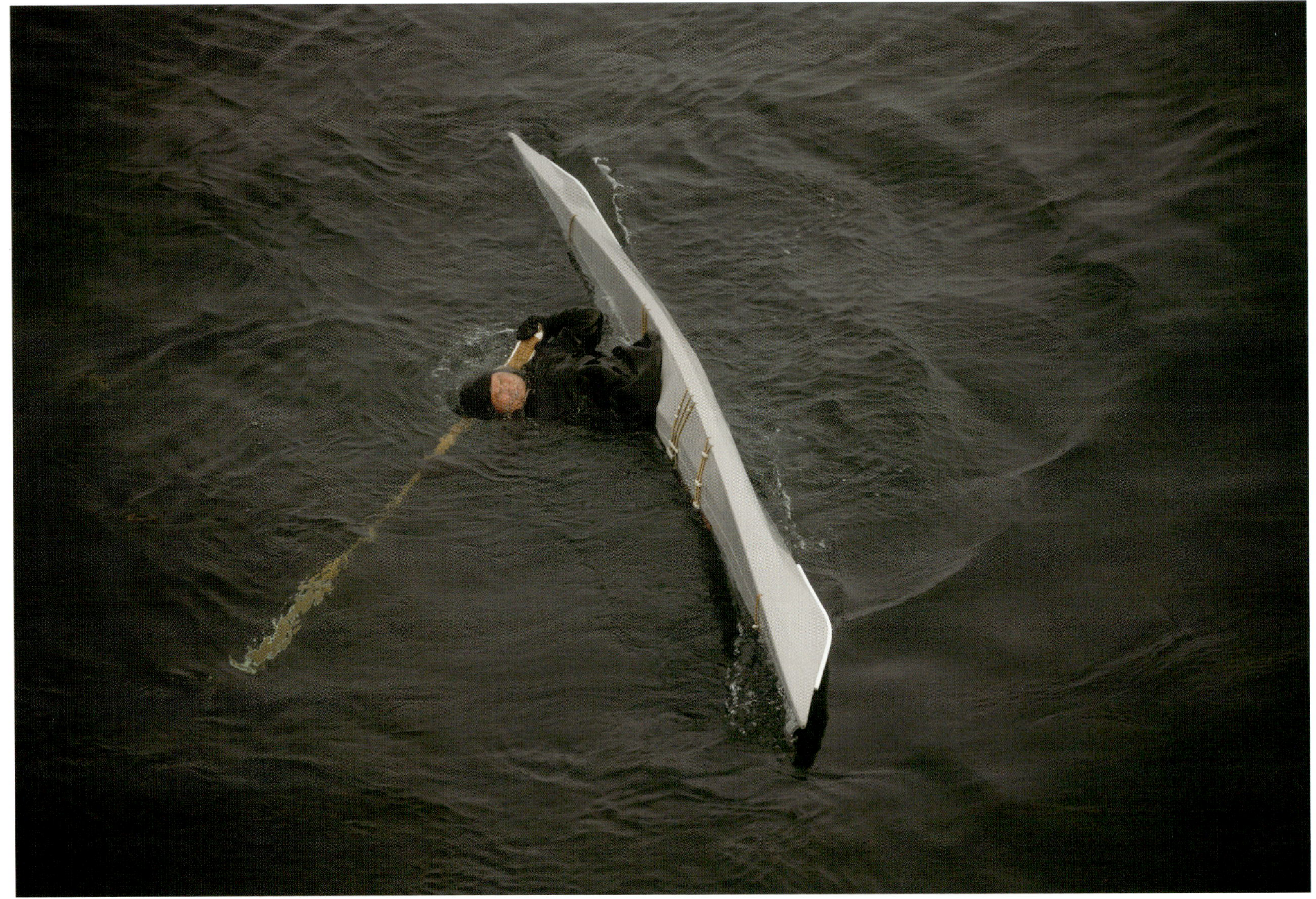

9. KAYAK ROLL, NUUK, GREENLAND

Water streaming across his face, a kayaker emerges from the cold steel-grey sea off Nuuk. In the past, with a lifestyle based on hunting and fishing, the kayak roll was an essential technique to master in the unforgiving waters of Greenland and the Canadian Arctic. Many still possess this consummate skill. Greenlanders are genetically and culturally descendants of a people known as Thule, who by the 16th century had settled along the whole length of the country's coast. They hunted seals and whales from kayaks with toggling harpoons attached to floats fashioned from sealskins.

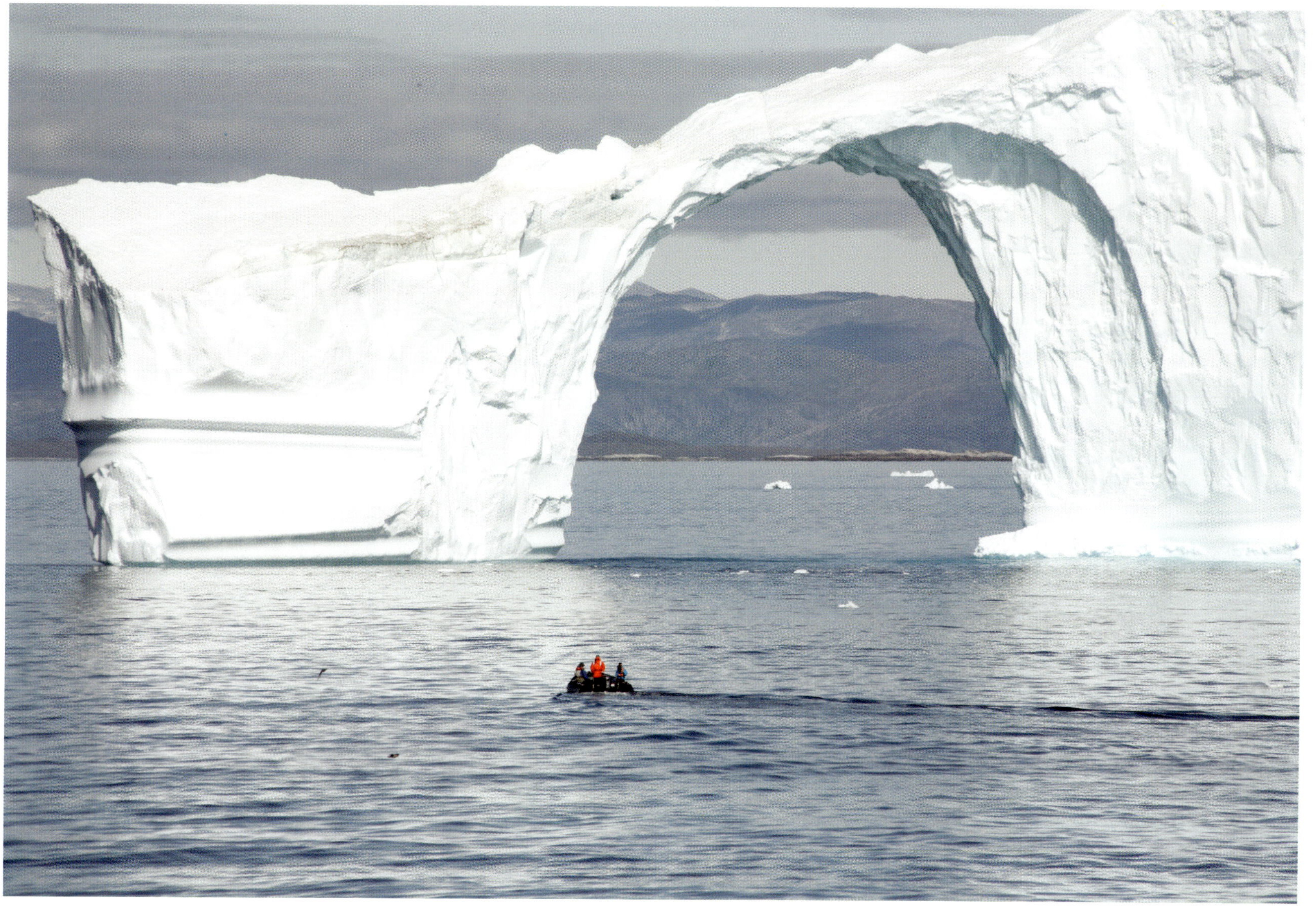

10. Iceberg Arch, Greenland

Fantastically sculpted by wave erosion and slowly melting in the heat from the sun, a huge iceberg has become grounded in shallow water. Originating from glaciers on the west coast of Greenland and in the Canadian Arctic, icebergs can drift for years. Caught in the Labrador Current large numbers are carried south into shipping lanes. It was one such iceberg that brought the maiden voyage of RMS Titanic to its tragic close on the night of 14 April 1912 with a huge loss of life. Of 2,223 passengers onboard, sadly 1,517 perished in the freezing waters of the North Atlantic.

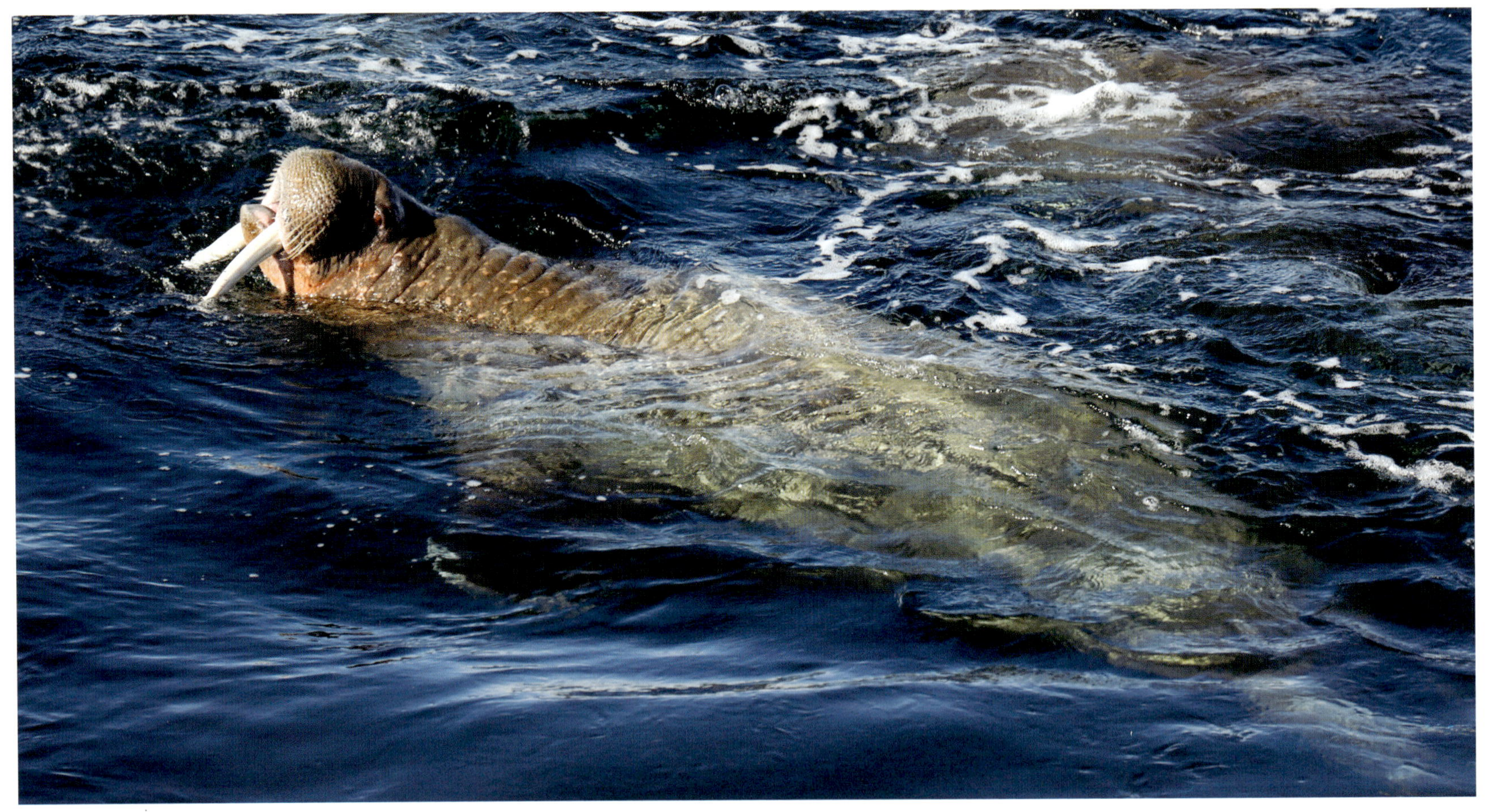

11. Walrus, Hamburgbukta, Spitsbergen, Svalbard

The walrus *(Odobenus rosmarus)* is found in shallow coastal waters in the Arctic. The word 'odobenus' means 'tooth-walker' and describes the habit of the animal hauling itself onto ice floes using its two tusks. They feed primarily on clams that live in the sediment on the seabed which they locate using highly sensitive vibrissae or whiskers, clearly seen on the snout of this individual. They suck the clams directly from their shells. Adults can weigh in at almost two tons. The name walrus is a derivation of 'valross', a Scandinavian word meaning 'whale-horse'. Its ivory tusks were traded in Europe by Viking merchants as raw material for the fashioning of high status objects such as chess pieces and items of jewellery.

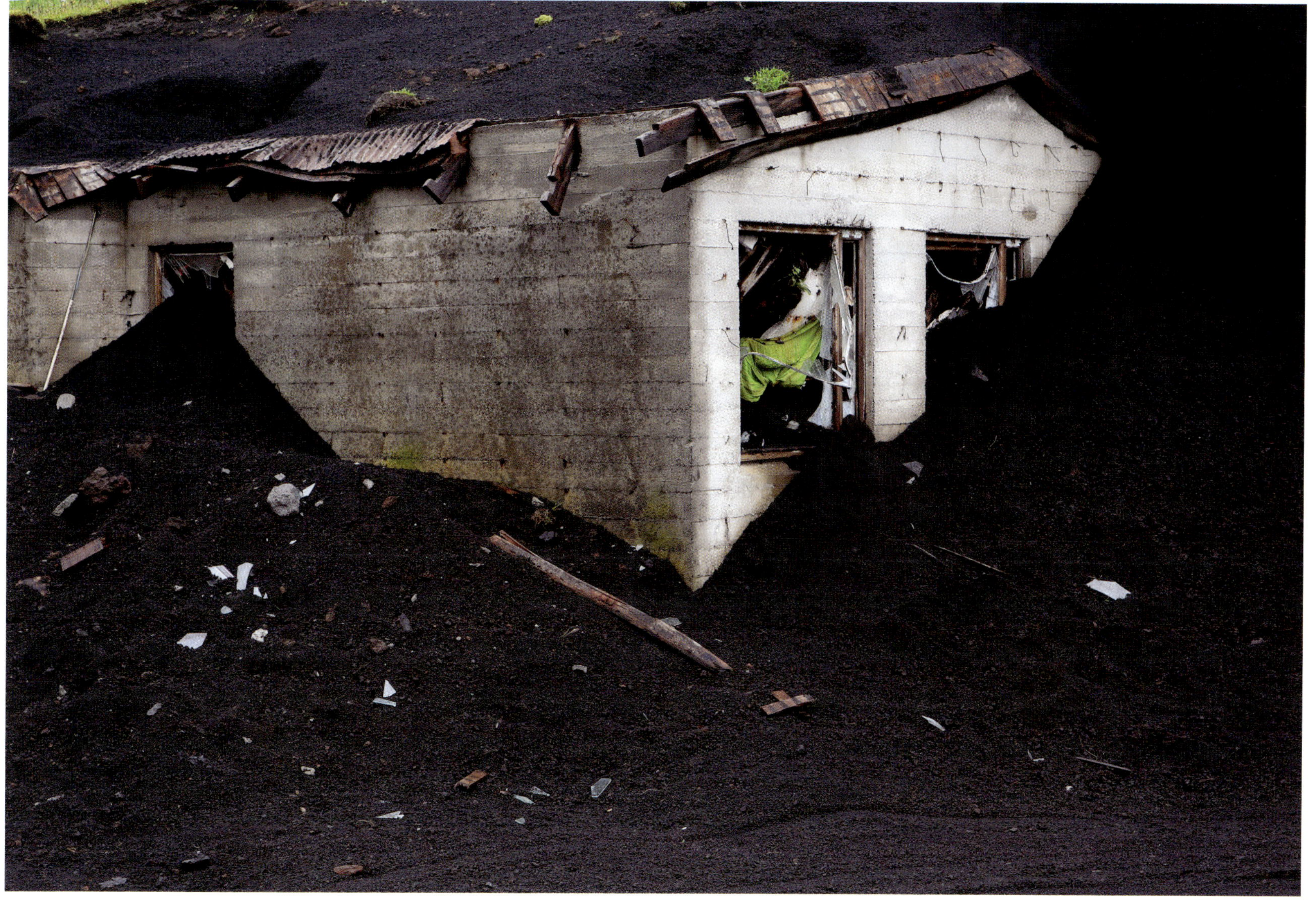

12. Pompeii of the North, Heimaey, Westmann Islands, Iceland

The shattered remains of a house encased in volcanic ash on the small island of Heimaey off the south coast of Iceland is a stark reminder of the power and unpredictability of Nature. In the early hours of 23 January 1973 a volcanic eruption began on the Eastern side of the island. The bulk of the town's 5,000 inhabitants were evacuated safely to the mainland on local fishing trawlers. Not a single person perished. Over the succeeding months almost a third of the houses and other buildings in the town were encased in thick deposits of tephra as the volcanic eruption continued unabated and is the reason why it is often called 'Pompeii of the North'.

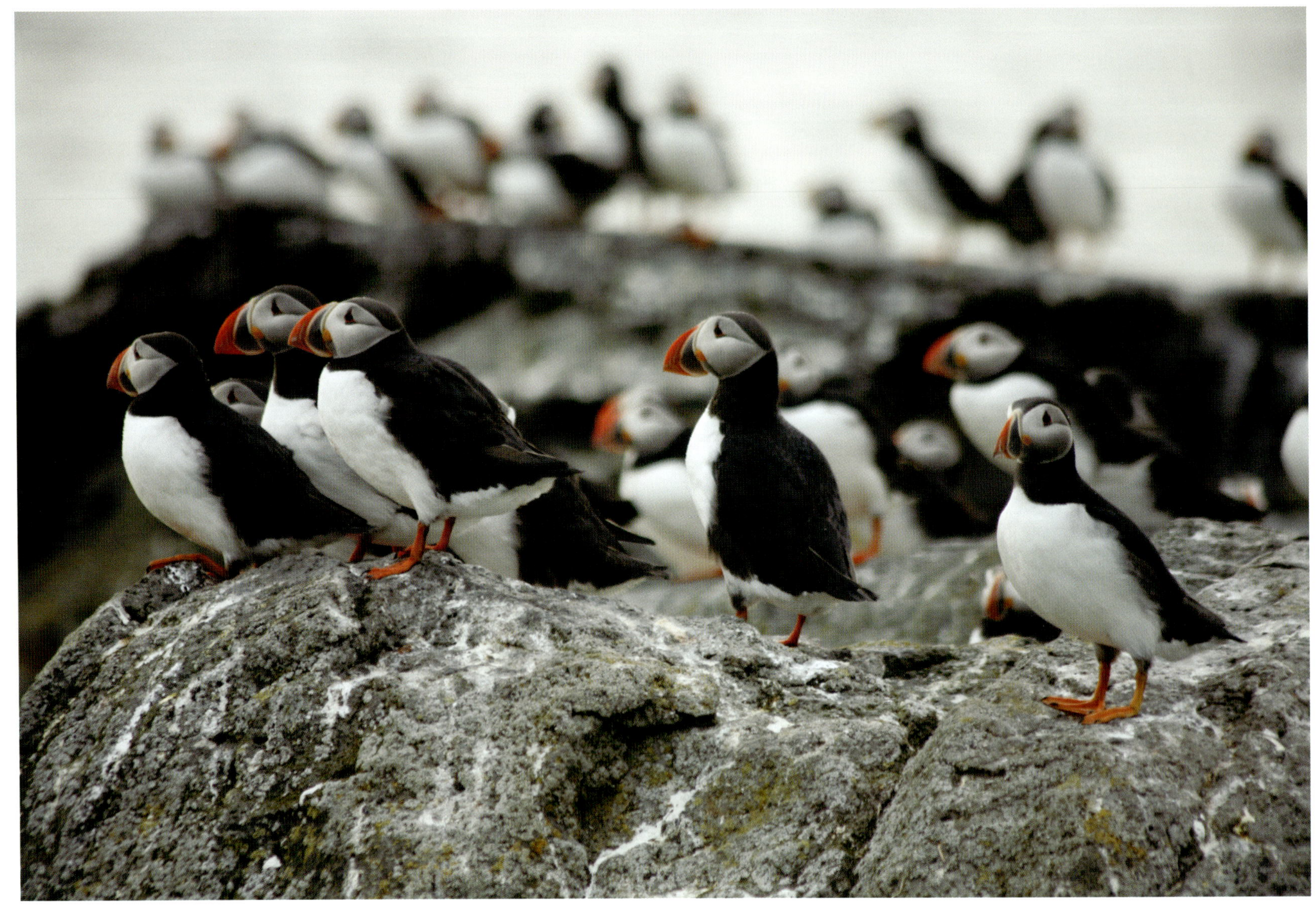

13. PUFFINS, VIGUR ISLAND, ISAFJORD, ICELAND

A large number of puffins come ashore to breed on Vigur Island. A single egg is laid in the chamber at the end of a long burrow. A member of the auk family, its Latin name, *Fratercula arctica,* is translated as 'Brother of the North'. The birds are highly gregarious by nature and often congregate in large 'rafts' on the water in summer. The large colourful beak is the origin of its nickname 'sea-parrot'. Puffins have been hunted for centuries in Iceland and are caught in a specialized net affixed to a 10 foot long wooden handle known as a *háfur.*

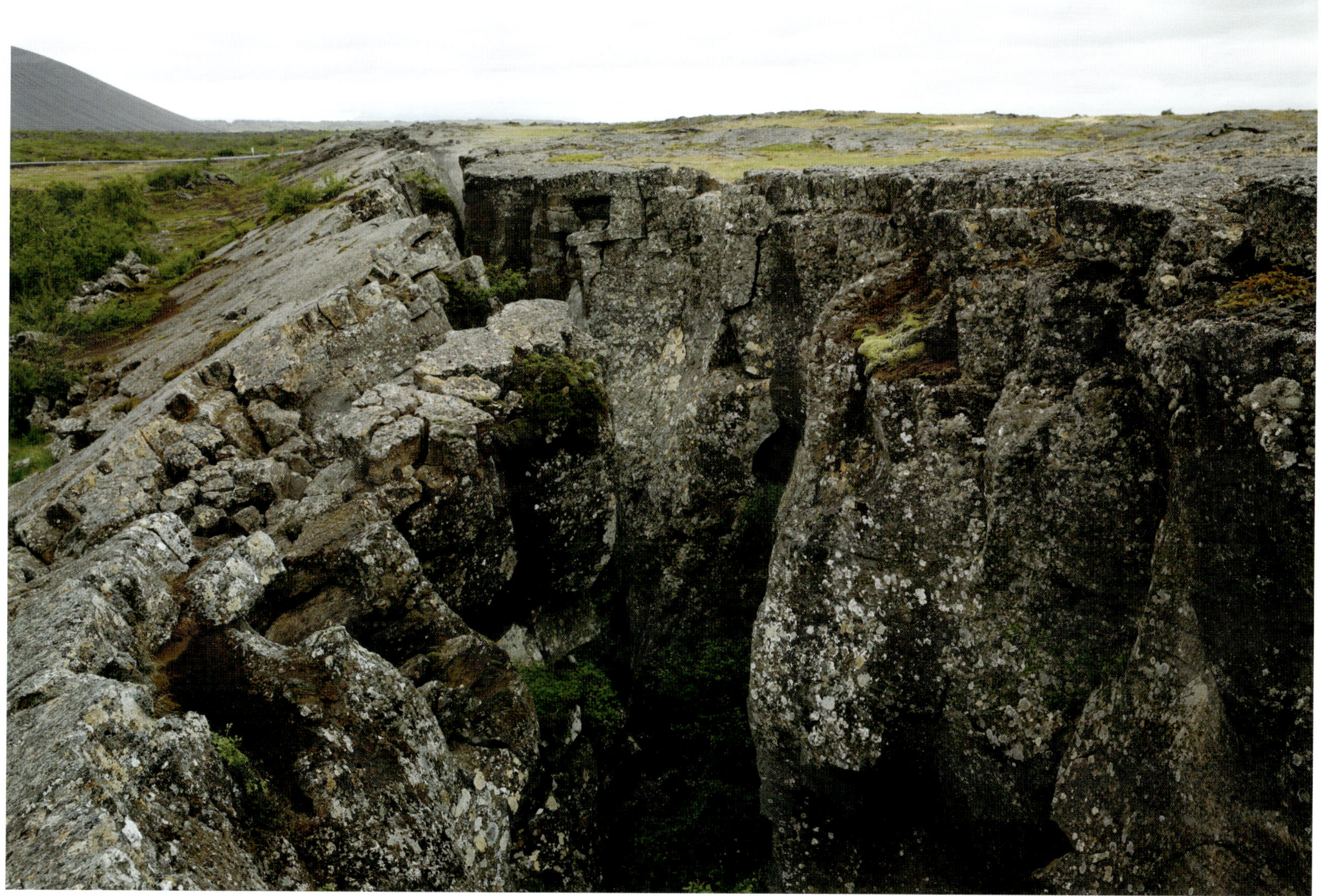

14. Tectonic Plates, Grjótagjá, Iceland

Iceland is a volcanic island that has formed from the buildup of incalculable quantities of magma over a period of approximately 24 million years. It lies astride the Mid-Atlantic Ridge, a sinuous submarine mountain chain. This geological feature forms the boundary between the North American and Eurasian tectonic plates. As these 'drift' apart, at an estimated rate of around an inch per year, Iceland is literally being slowly torn apart. The effects of this can be seen at several locations including Grjótagjá ('Rock Chasm') and Thingvellir ('Assembly Plains').

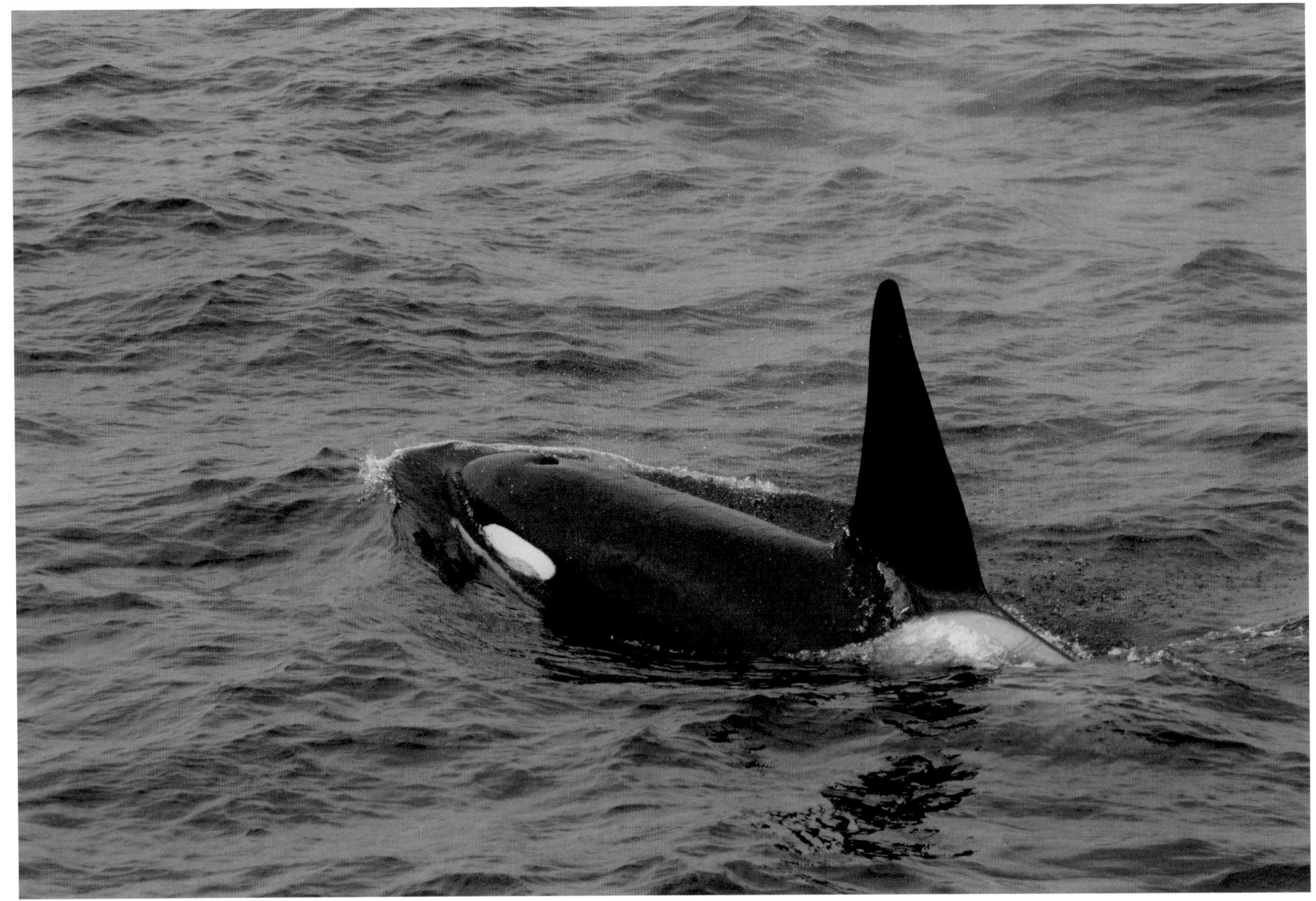

15 Male Killer Whale, Westmann Islands, Iceland

A male killer whale cleaves the waters close to the Westmann Islands. The largest species of dolphin in the world, it is easily recognizable by its jet-black body, white underparts and eye patch and grey saddle-patch. A toothed whale, this highly efficient predato takes a variety of prey including seals, sharks, seabirds, squid and other whales. They usually form closely-knit family pods of between 5 and 20 members and often hunt collectively. The dorsal fin can grow to 6 feet in height in adult males. Its name derives from whalers in the 18th century who observed them feeding on other cetaceans.

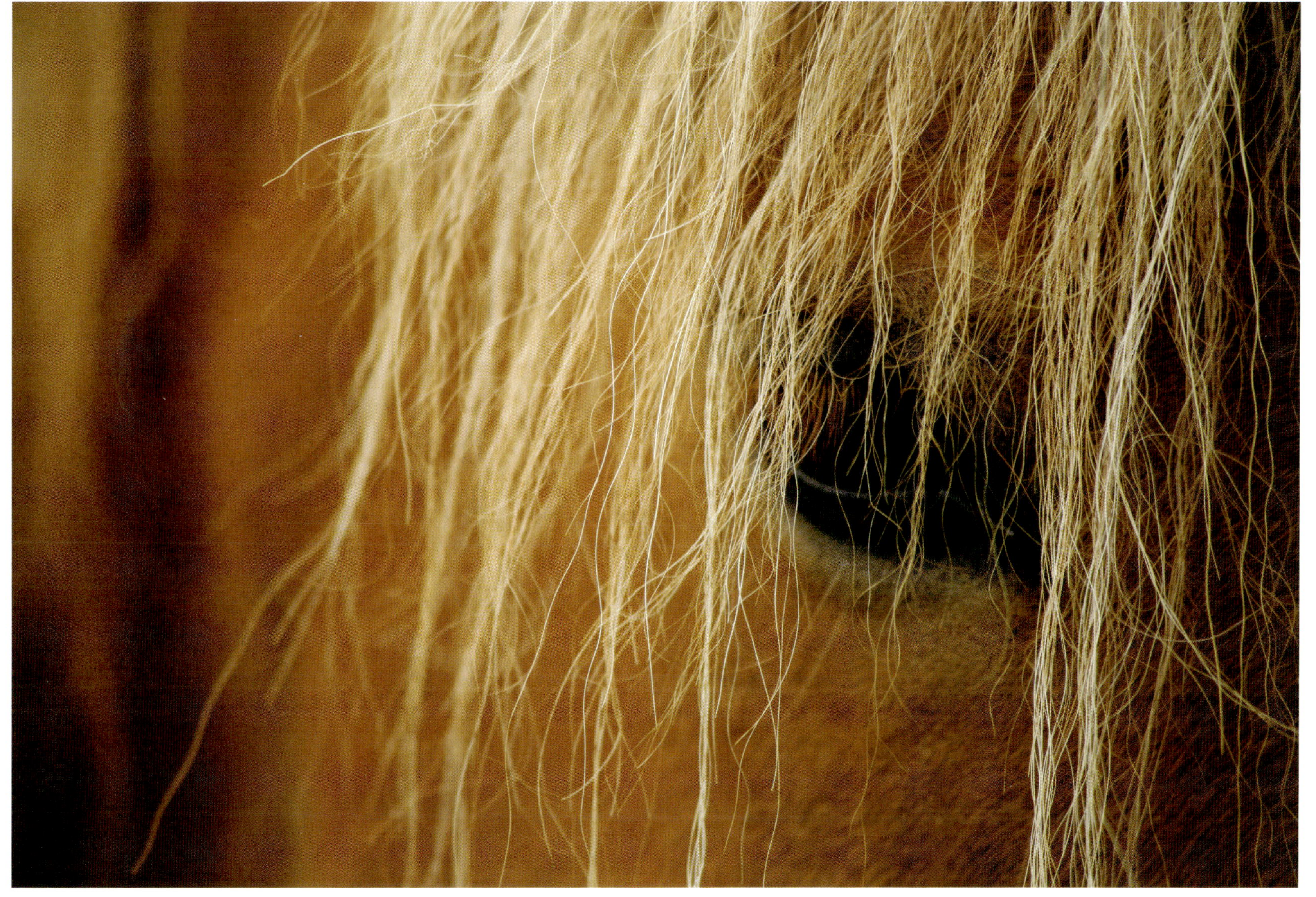

16. Icelandic Horse, Hveragerdi, Iceland

Norse Viking chieftains first established settlements in Iceland in the late 9th century. They brought with them a small, stocky and surefooted breed of horse which has remained virtually unchanged since then. Extremely popular, this is now known as the Icelandic horse. In the past it was the only mode of transport in a country where roads and bridges were not well-developed. The breed is now stringently safeguarded by governmental regulation which ensures that it remains pure. This includes a ban on the importation of other horses into Iceland.

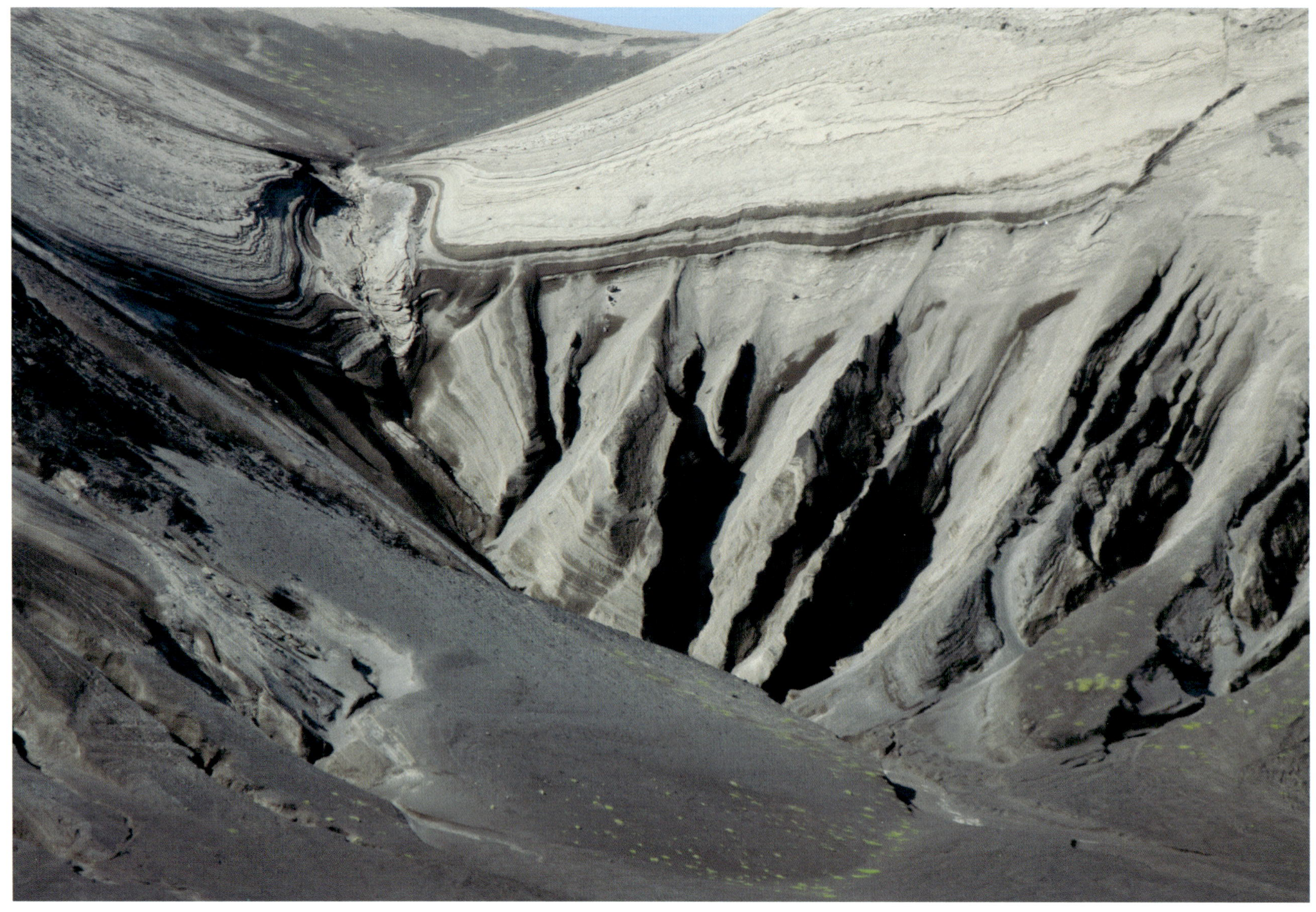

17. Surtsey, Westmann Islands, Iceland

The youngest of the Westmann Islands by far, Surtsey formed during a four-year long volcanic eruption which started on the seabed. The first to witness the spectacle were some fishermen who initially observed smoke and steam rising from the water on 14 November 1963. By the following day a small island had already formed. The eruption came to a close in June 1967. The new volcanic island was named after the Norse fire giant Surtur. A nature reserve, Surtsey is now an open air research laboratory where scientists are studying the complex mechanisms of plant and animal colonization and ecosystem development. It was listed as a UNESCO World Heritage Site in 2008

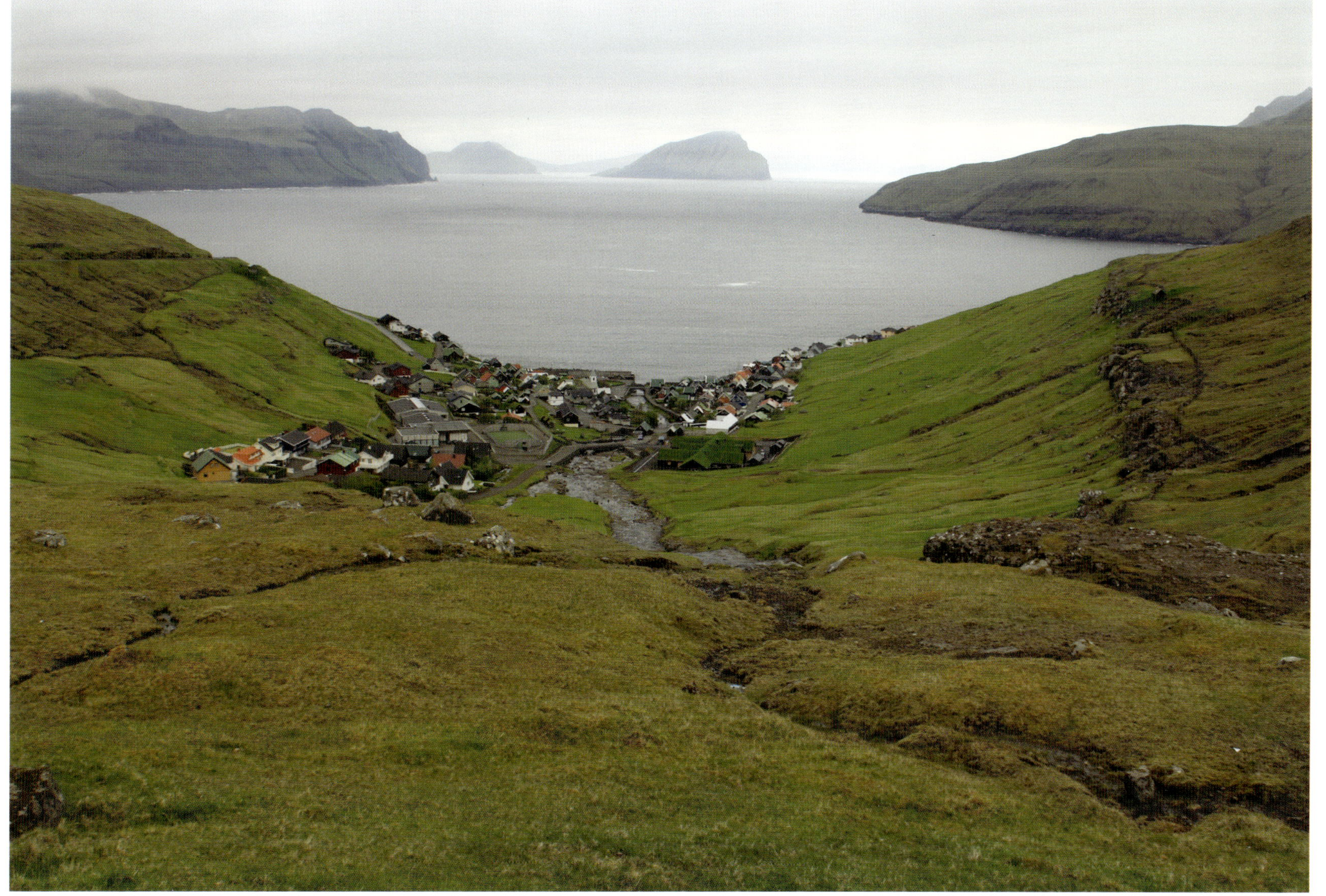

18. Kvivik, Streymoy, Faeroes

The Faeroes appear to have been used as a retreat by Irish monks for over a century prior to their settlement by Norwegian Vikings in the 9th century. Archaeological excavations in 1941 in the small village of Kvivik, on Streymoy, revealed the remains of a Viking period farm consisting of a longhouse and byre side by side. In the former the remains of a kerbed central fireplace and raised seating-cum-bedding benches made of soil along its sidewalls were noted. The byre had a number of stalls to accommodate cattle. The site seems to have been chosen for settlement because of the protected nature of the small bay and good grazing for livestock. The pattern of small hayfields is a legacy of the original Norse farmers.

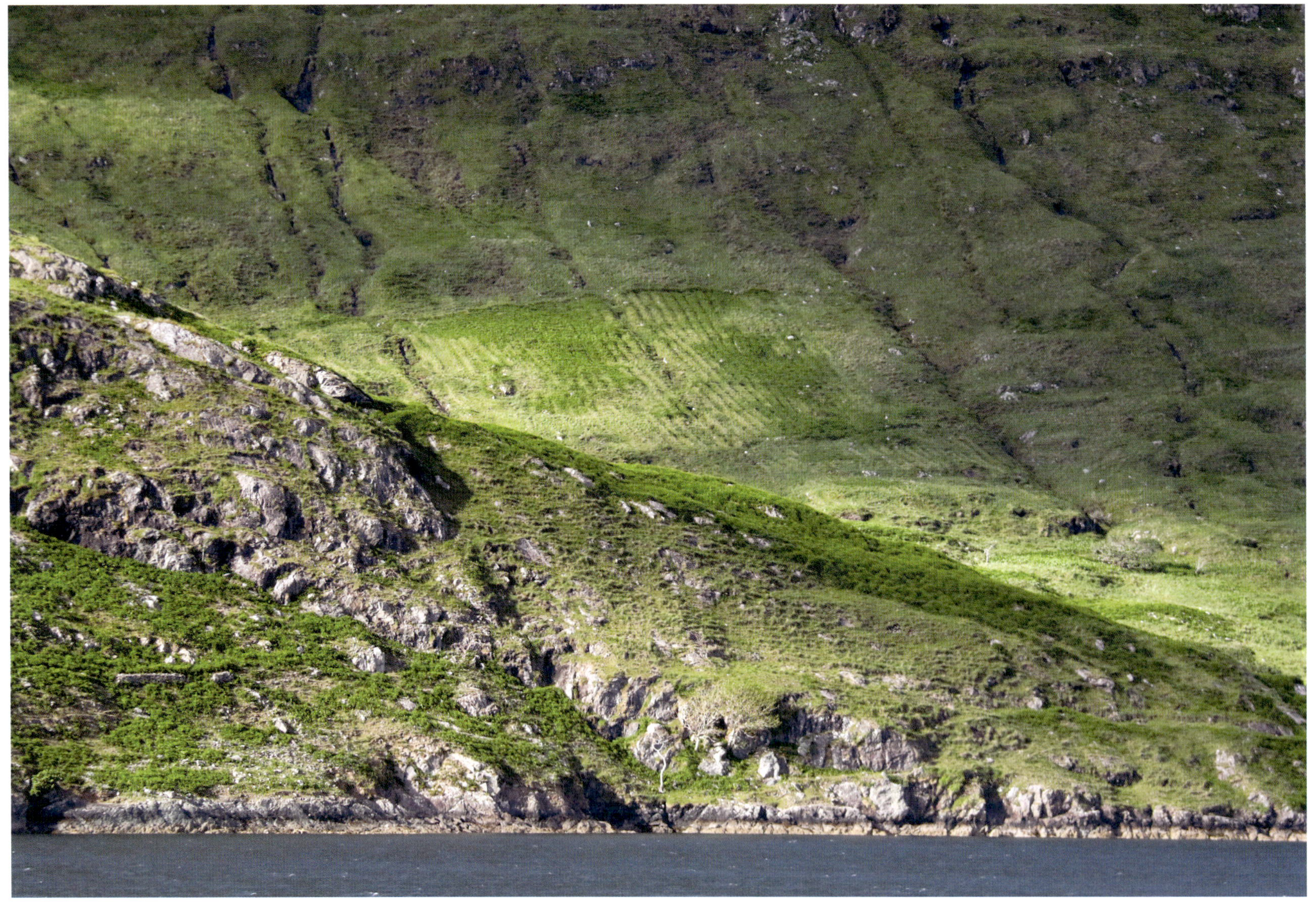

19. Lazy Beds, Killary Harbour, Galway, Ireland

Bathed in late evening light, abandoned lazy-beds on the slopes of Killary Harbour are a reminder of one of the great watersheds in Irish history. Introduced in the 1580s, the potato had by the mid-19th century become the staple of the bulk of the population of this island. An estimated 5.4 million people were totally dependent on it. The average farm labourer ate between 12 and 16 lbs. of potatoes every day. The type was known as a lumper or horse potato and was particularly susceptible to the blight, *Phytopthora infestans,* which was first observed in the Botanic Gardens in Dublin in August 1845. In that year there were an estimated 2.5 million acres planted with potatoes. They were grown on so-called lazy beds all along the western and southwestern seaboard and in upland areas throughout the countryside.

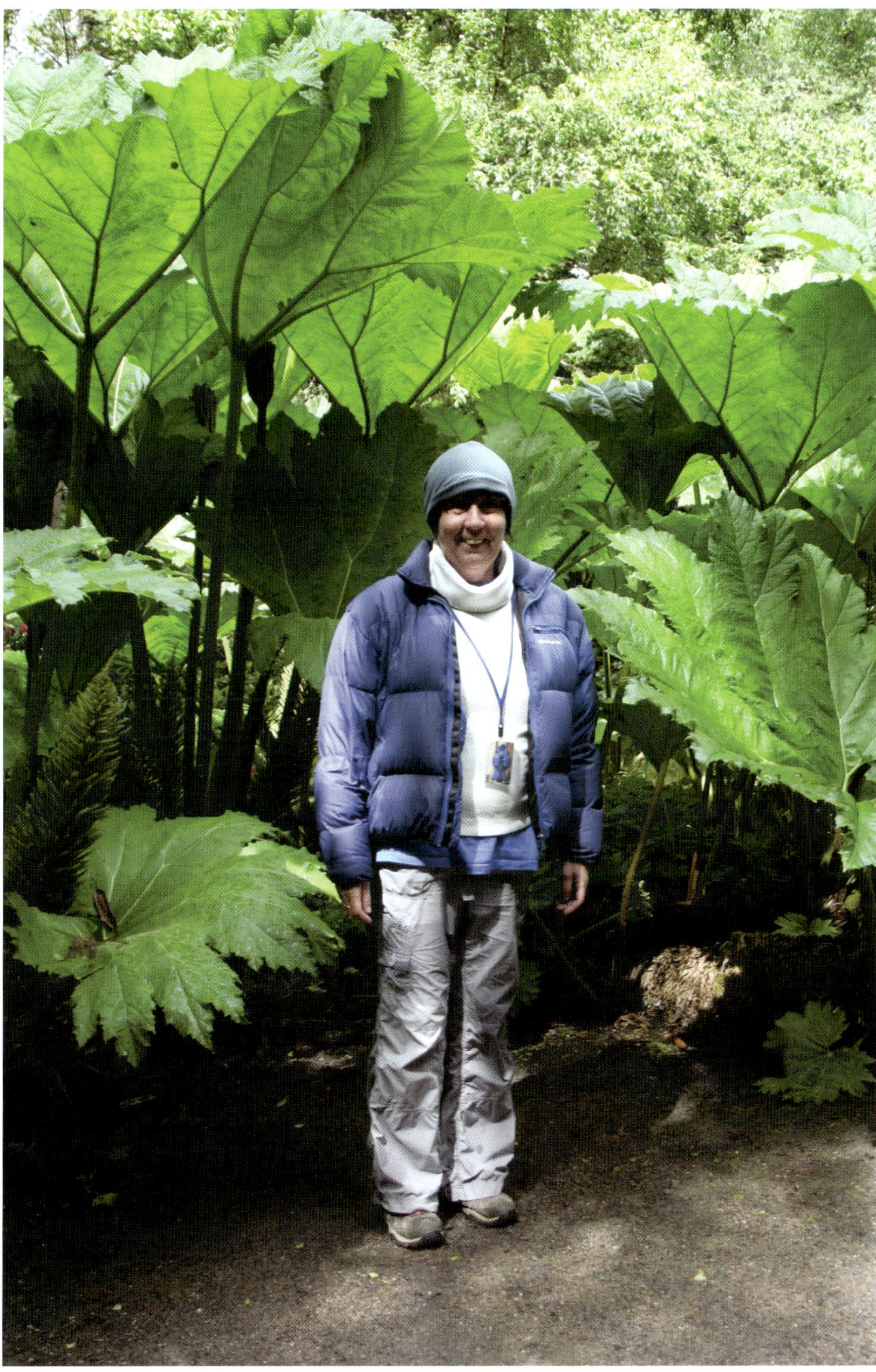

20. Lindi and Gunnera, Inverewe Gardens, Scotland

My wife Lindi kindly doubles up as a scale to give an indication of the impressive proportions of a gunnera plant growing in the Inverewe Gardens. A native of Brazil, this particular species is *Gunnera manicata*. Its leaves can be 4 feet wide and heights of 8 feet are typical. It was introduced as an ornamental plant to embellish gardens and is known by a variety of names including Brazilian Giant Rhubarb and Dinosaur Food. The Inverewe Gardens are tucked away on the shores of Loch Ewe on the north-west coast of Scotland. The warming effect of the Gulf Stream allows a range of exotic subtropical plants to flourish here.

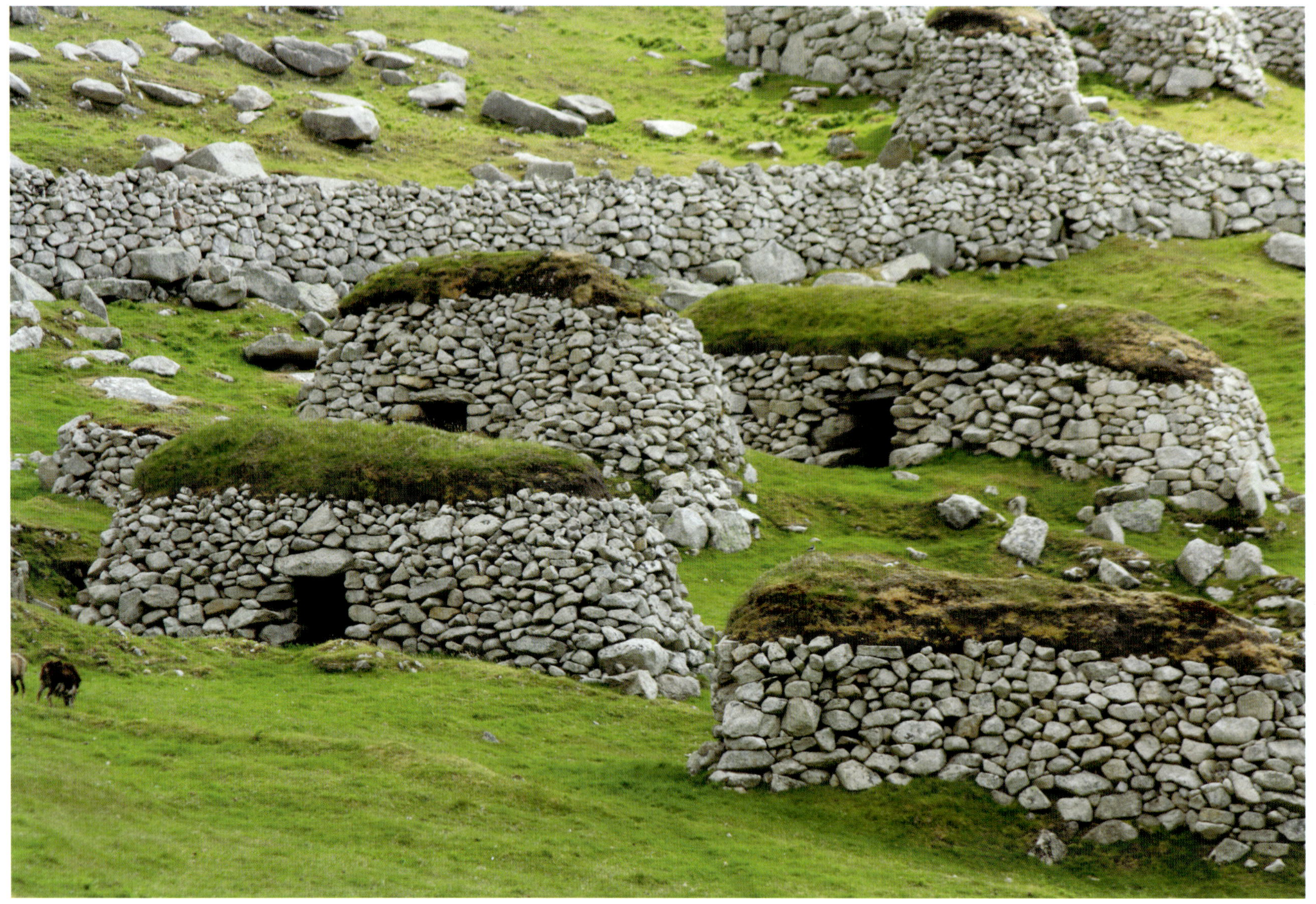

21. Cleits, Hirta, St Kilda, Outer Hebrides, Scotland

Cleits are corbelled drystone storehouses unique to St Kilda, a small archipelago 110 miles off the western coast of Scotland in the Outer Hebrides. Life here was dependent on the annual harvesting of seabirds and their eggs from its vertiginous cliffs. The most important was the fulmar which provided meat, oil and feathers. In August fowlers were lowered on a rope from the cliff top down to the rock ledges below. The fulmars were then snatched and dispatched as they carefully worked their way along the line of nests. Plucked and cleaned, they were stored in the cleits where the wind passing through the gaps in the walls dried them. These were eaten throughout the winter. The last 36 inhabitants of a once thriving community were evacuated from Hirta in August 1930.

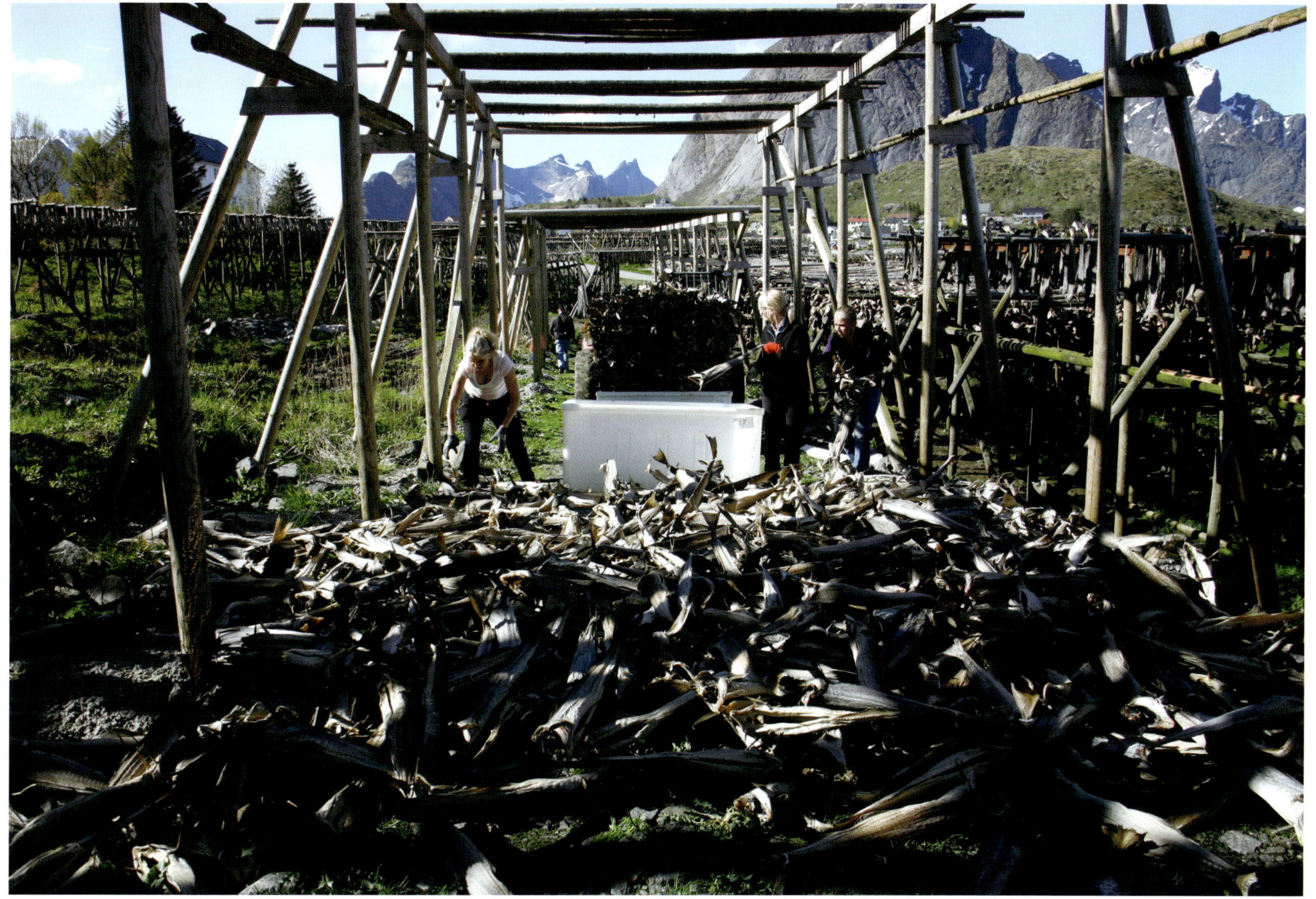

22. Processing Cod, Reine, Lofoten Islands, Norway

Dried cod is loaded in preparation for export to Nigeria in the small town of Reine. Between January and April massive numbers of cod are fished in the rich waters offshore. They are split and hung in serried ranks on wooden racks to dry. The Lofoten Islands were for centuries the most important cod fishery in Norway. The dried fish, known as stockfish, were shipped south to Bergen and exchanged for much needed provisions including rye, flour, salt and tobacco. There was a huge demand for stockfish in Europe during a time when Roman Catholics had to abstain from eating red meat on Fridays and numerous other Feastdays

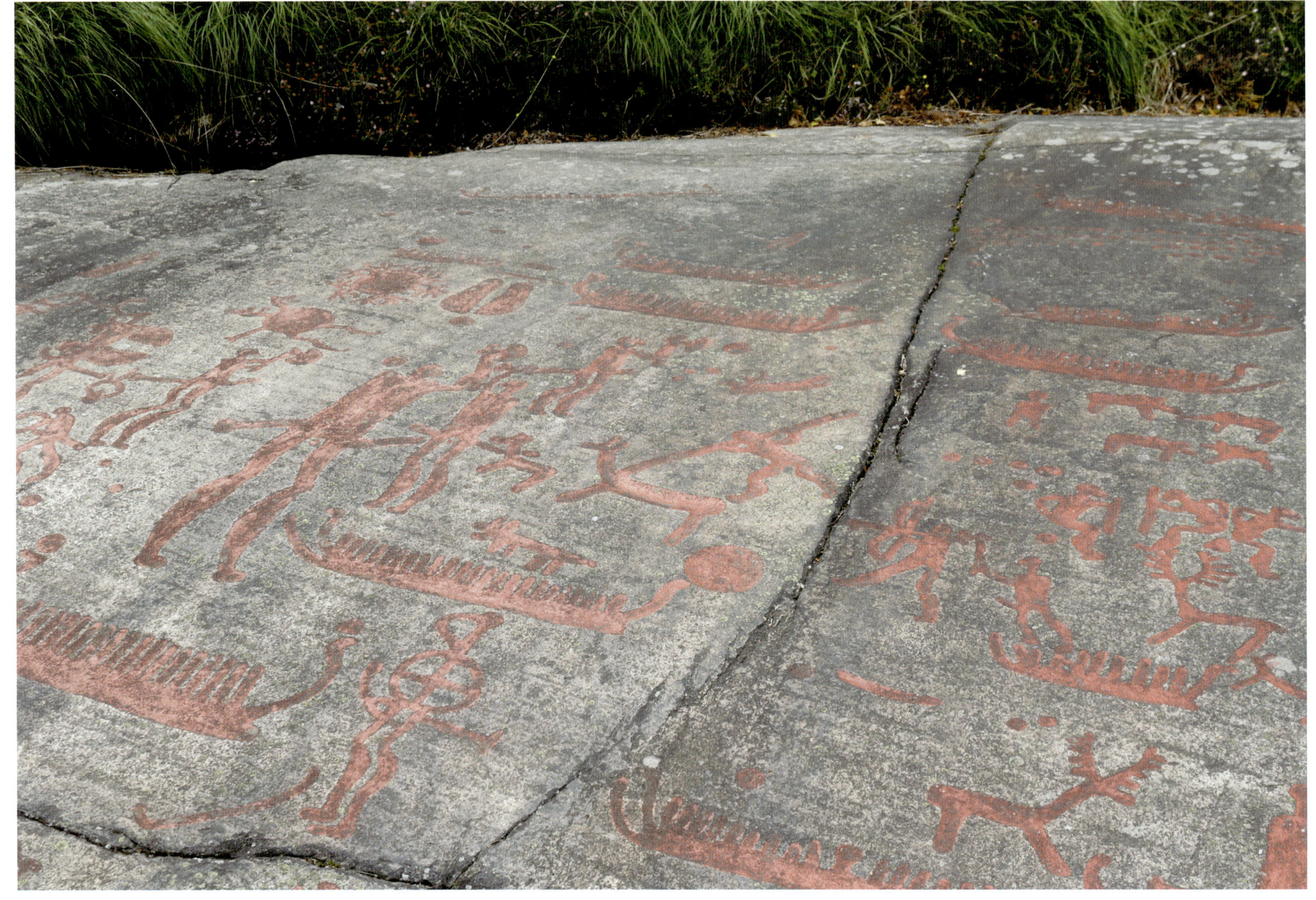

23. Rock Carvings, Grebbestad, Tanum, Sweden

Prehistoric artists chose this large glacier-smoothed granite outcrop as their canvas. Using stone tools they pecked a wide range of figures and symbols into its surface sometime around 2,000 BC. These include humans, boats, and chariots. Scenes of ploughing, herding and hunting provide glimpses of the daily life of a long-vanished culture. The carvings have recently been highlighted with red paint. In the Tanum area there are close to 600 known petroglyph sites which combined are decorated with tens of thousands of individual carvings. It was designated a UNESCO World Heritage Site in 1994.

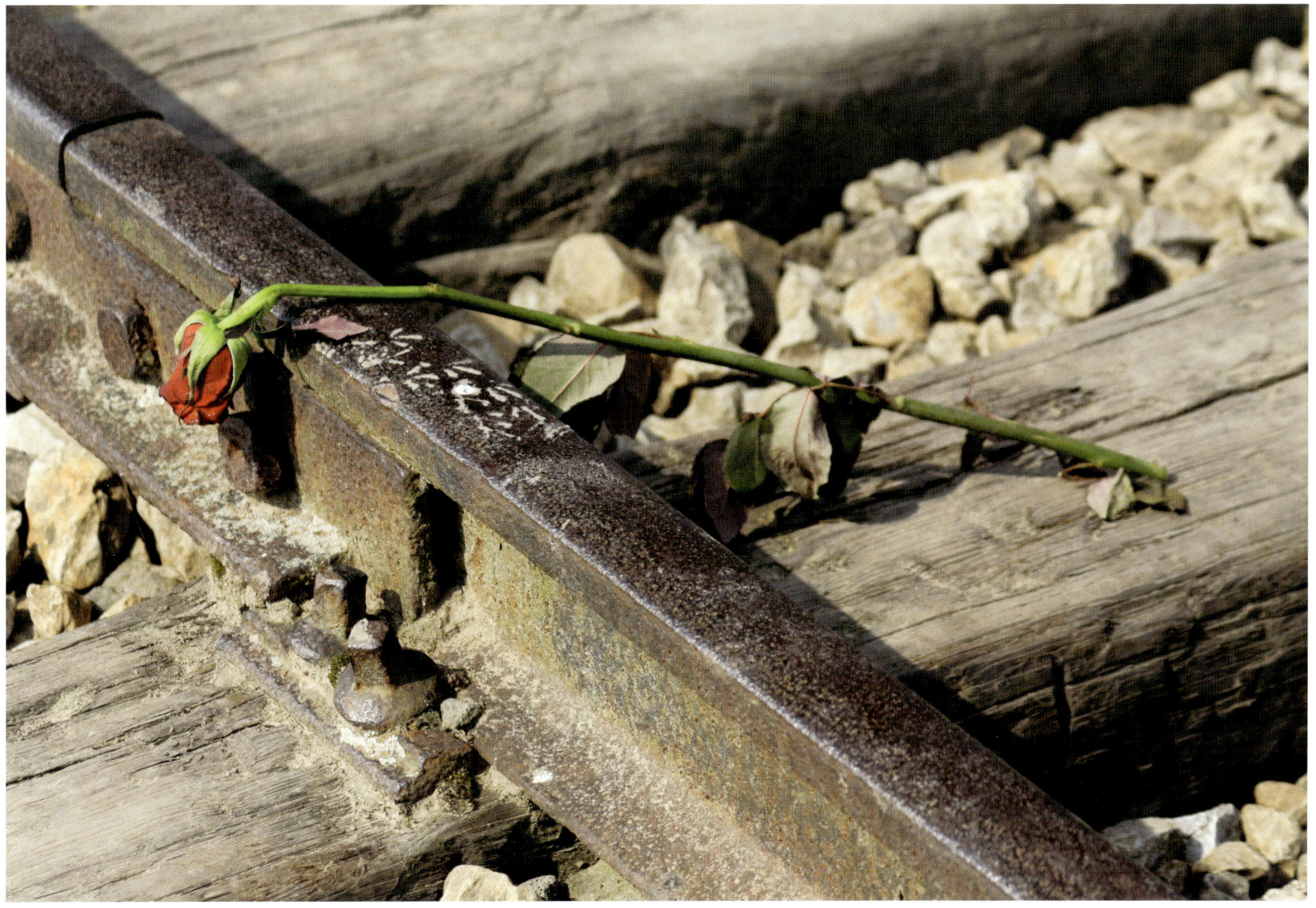

24. Floral Tribute, Auschwitz II-Birkenau, Poland

A rose lies across a rail track at Birkenau in sad remembrance of the large scale murder here of Jewish people during the Second World War. Originally functioning solely as a concentration camp, in 1942 Auschwitz was extended with the construction of what was to become known as Auschwitz II-Birkenau. This new complex acted primarily as an extermination centre for European Jews. Over 1 million were transported here in 1944 alone. Once disembarked from the train carriages the new arrivals were subjected to the terrifying ordeal of 'selection' by members of the SS on the adjoining platforms. Those who were deemed unfit for work by camp doctors – the old, the sick, children, pregnant women – were immediately escorted to the nearby gas chambers where they were then systematically murdered and incinerated in the camp's crematoria.

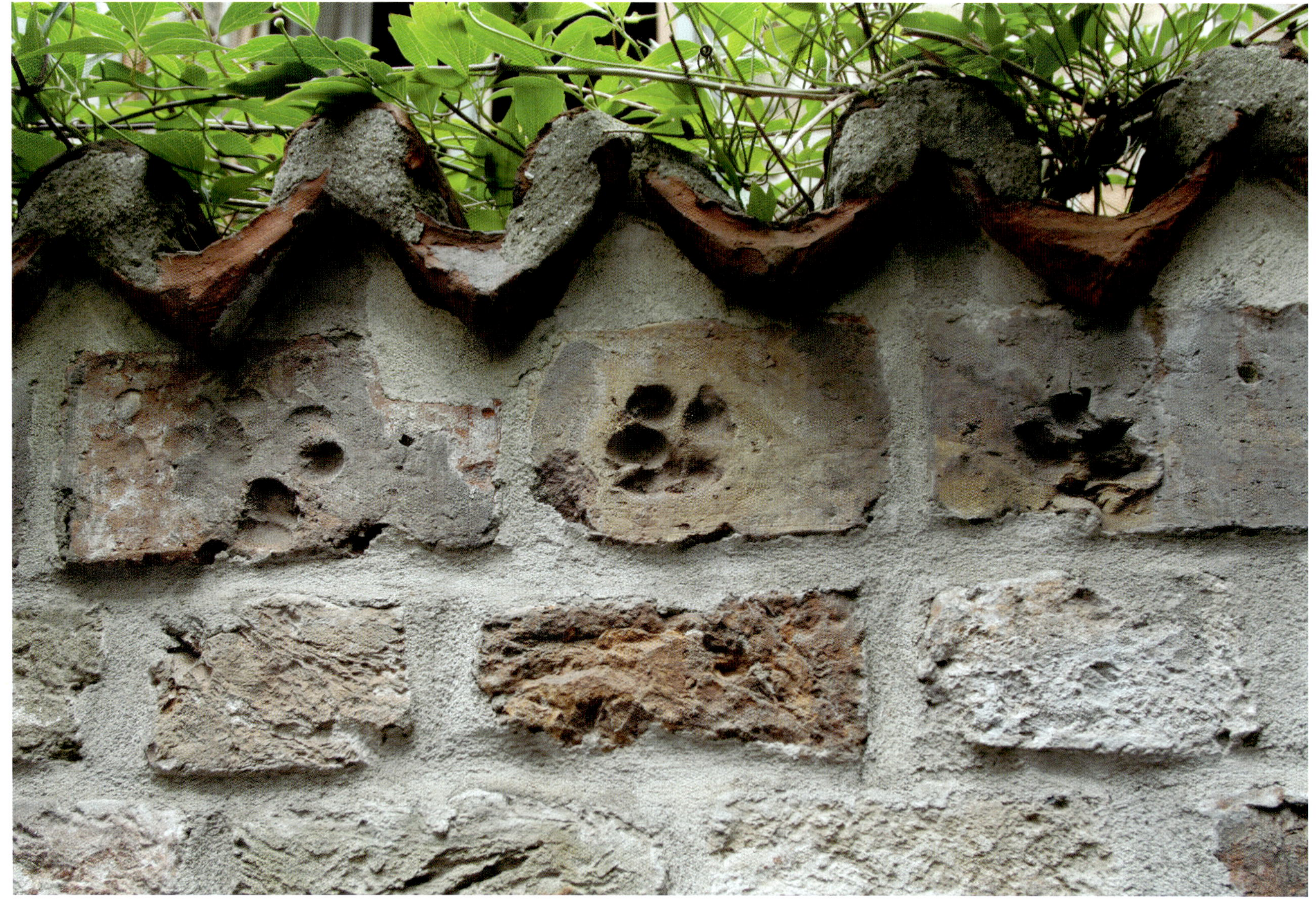

25. Medieval Dog Paw Prints, Lubeck, Germany

The Hanseatic League, a commercial confederation of North German merchant cities, was founded in the 13th century. With Lubeck as its capital, it monopolized the maritime trade of the Baltic and North Sea. By the 15th century its commercial success was expressed in extensive urban development, funded by a wealthy merchant class. Warehouses, city fortifications, town houses, cathedrals and town halls were constructed in brick. Occasionally paw marks were imprinted by a passing dog or cat in the soft clay of bricks being made in open moulds at the brickworks. Lubeck has been listed as a UNESCO World Heritage Site because of its brick-rich architecture.

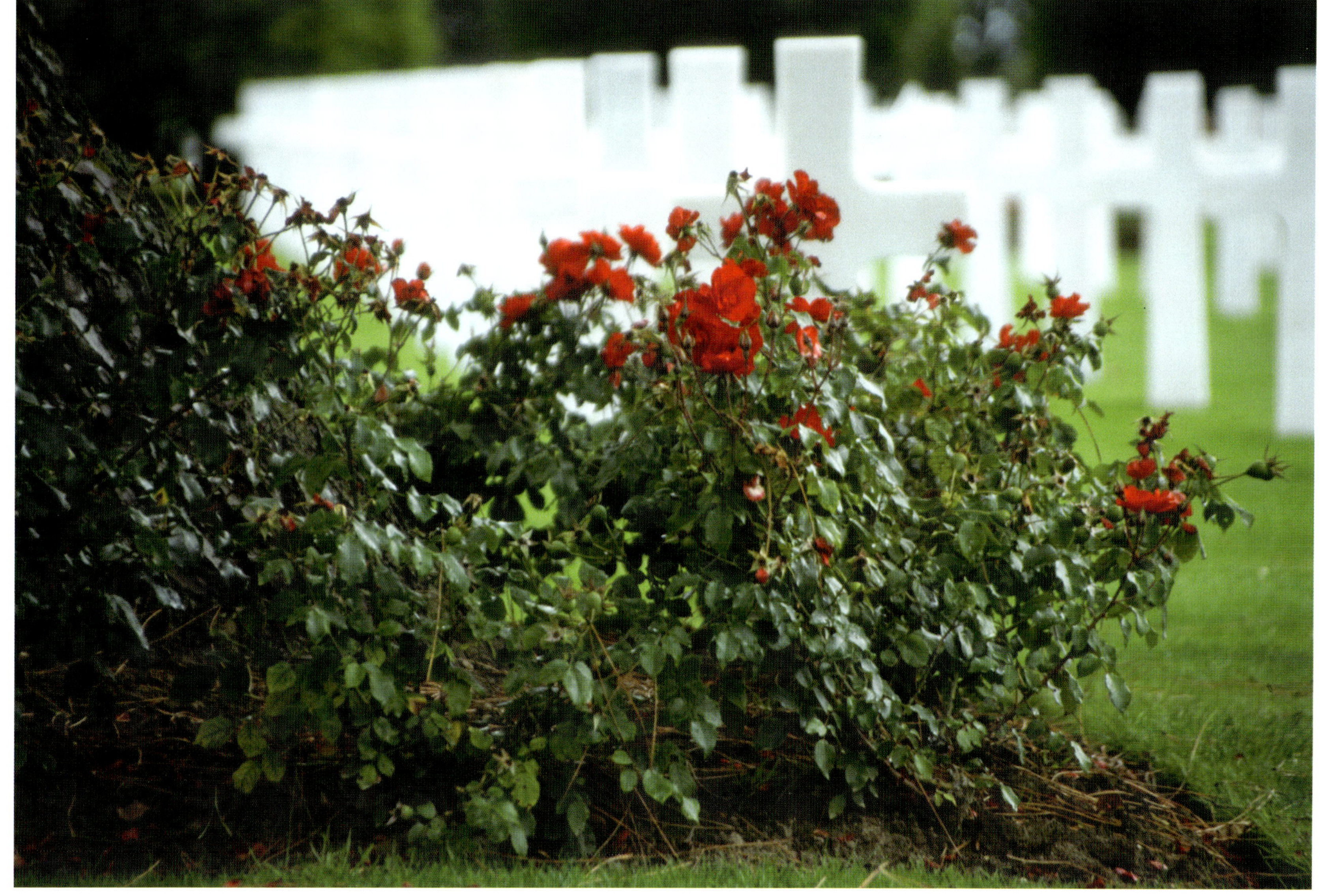

26. British Commonwealth Cemetery, Bayeux, France

On 6 June1944 the now famous D-Day landings on the beaches of Normandy began at 6.30 am when the first wave of American troops came ashore at 'Utah' and 'Omaha'. The Allied 'Overlord' offensive in North-Western Europe had begun. The campaign fought in Normandy is regarded by many as the crucial battle of the Second World War. Tenacious defense by German forces and the ensuing intense fighting ensured a massive loss of life. The largest Commonwealth Second World War cemetery in France is located in Bayeux, a town famous for its remarkable Medieval tapestry. It contains over 4,000 Commonwealth and hundreds of German soldiers graves.

27. Resting Pilgrims, Santiago De Compostella, Spain

The culmination of a walk begun several months earlier in Rome is celebrated by two newly arrived pilgrims enjoying a well-earned break in this sun-drenched plaza in Santiago de Compostella. The scallop shell affixed to their hats is the symbol associated with this venerated site. The region of Galicia is crisscrossed by ancient pilgrim routes used by devotees from many Europe countries since the Middle Ages. Their confluence lies at one of the most iconic religious sites in Christendom, namely the tomb of St. James the Apostle in the cathedral in Santiago de Compostella. His remains rest in an ornately decorated chest in the crypt beneath the main altar.

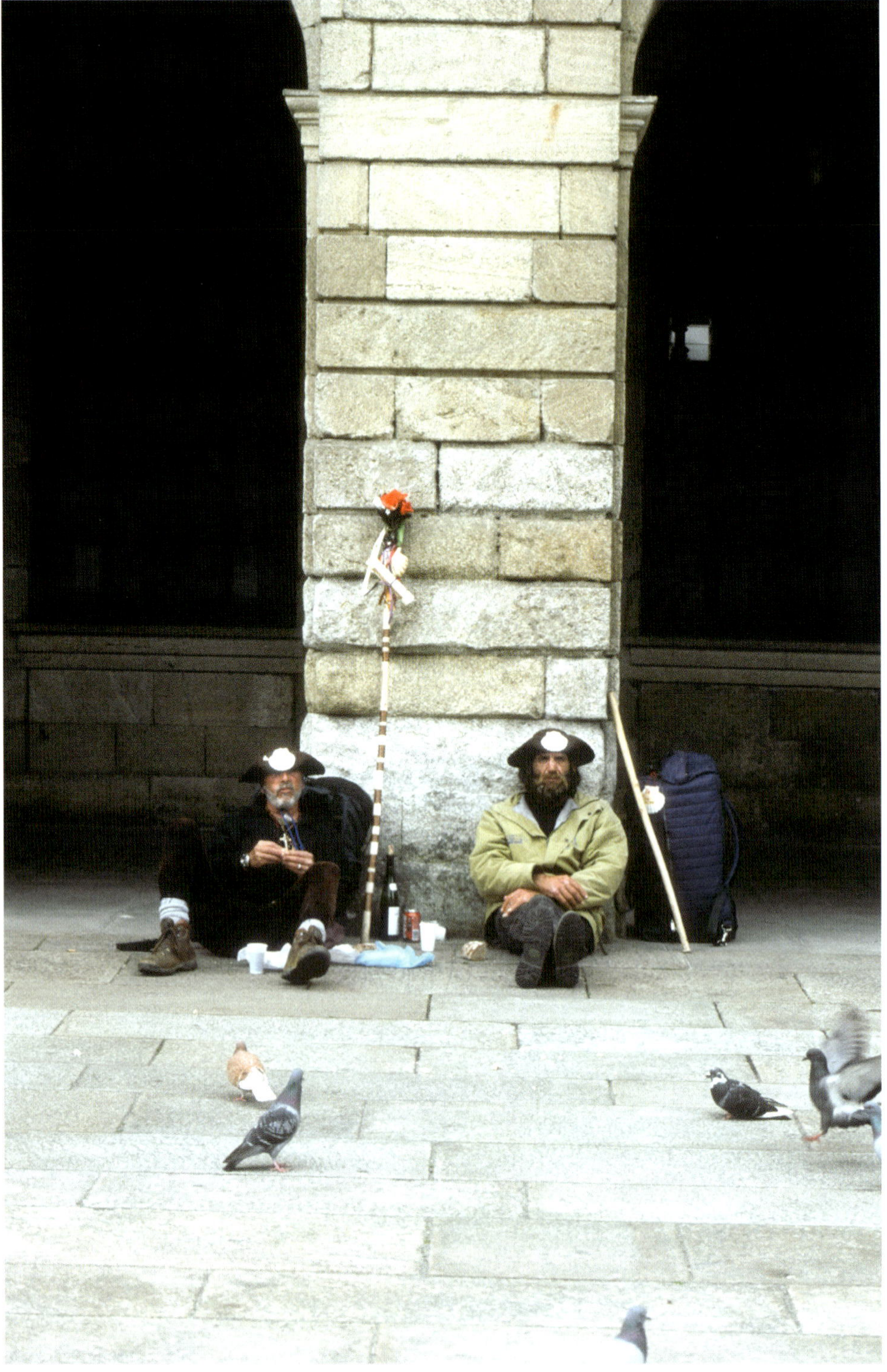

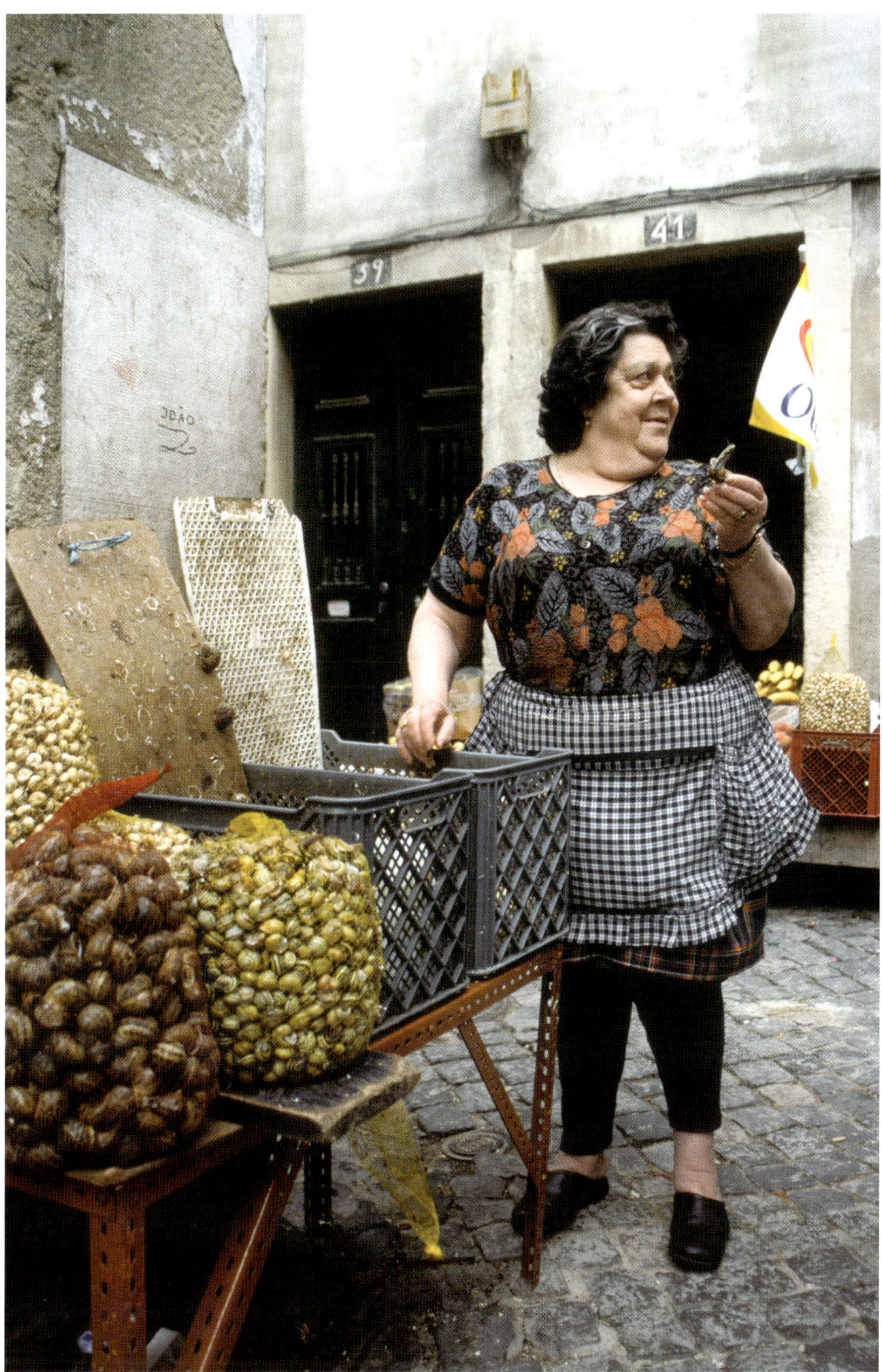

28. Snail Seller, Lisbon, Portugal

A smiling street vendor proffers a snail to a passer-by in a laneway in Lisbon. One of the most traditional Portuguese dishes is caracois - the humble snail. Cooked in garlic and oregano it is a very popular summer snack, particularly in Lisbon and the South. They are readily available in food markets and can be purchased from any number of street vendors. Ever popular international and local snail festivals are held in towns and villages throughout the summer. Portuguese, Spanish, Moroccan and French chefs come to cook snails. These gatherings are also opportunities to showcase the country's rich cultural heritage in cuisine, music, song, and dance.

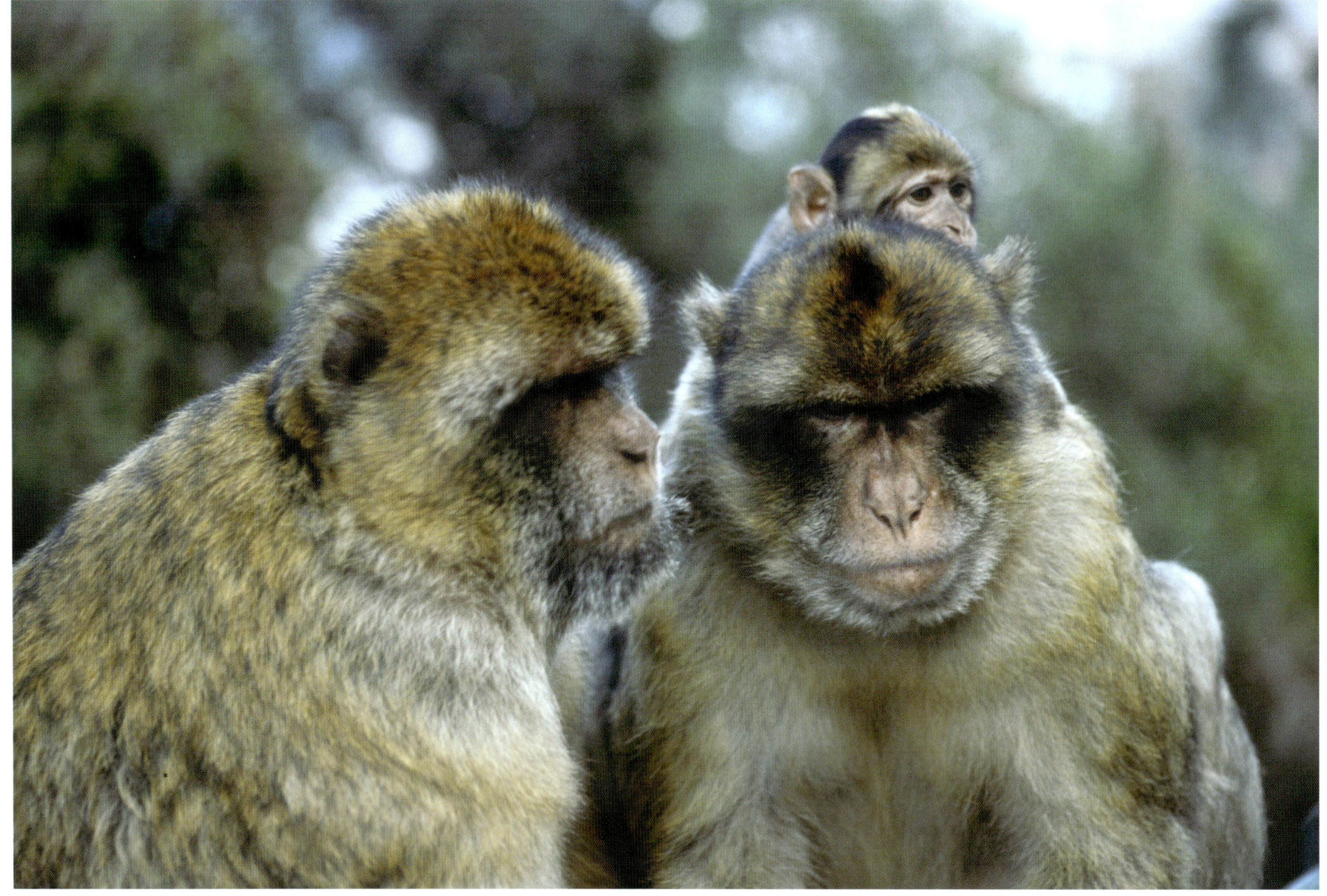

29. Macaque Monkeys, Gibraltar

The so-called barbary apes, like this family group, that tourists flock to the Rock of Gibraltar to photograph are in fact tailless macaque monkeys. Tough, adaptable and capable of enduring cold conditions, they are found living in the wild in the cedar forests of the Atlas Mountains in nearby Morocco. There are several theories as to how the monkeys first arrived in Gibraltar. It is possible that they were originally brought over as pets by the Moors from the early 8th century onwards and then later became feral. The present troop has been replenished several times, under the auspices of the local British authorities, from the native stock in Morocco.

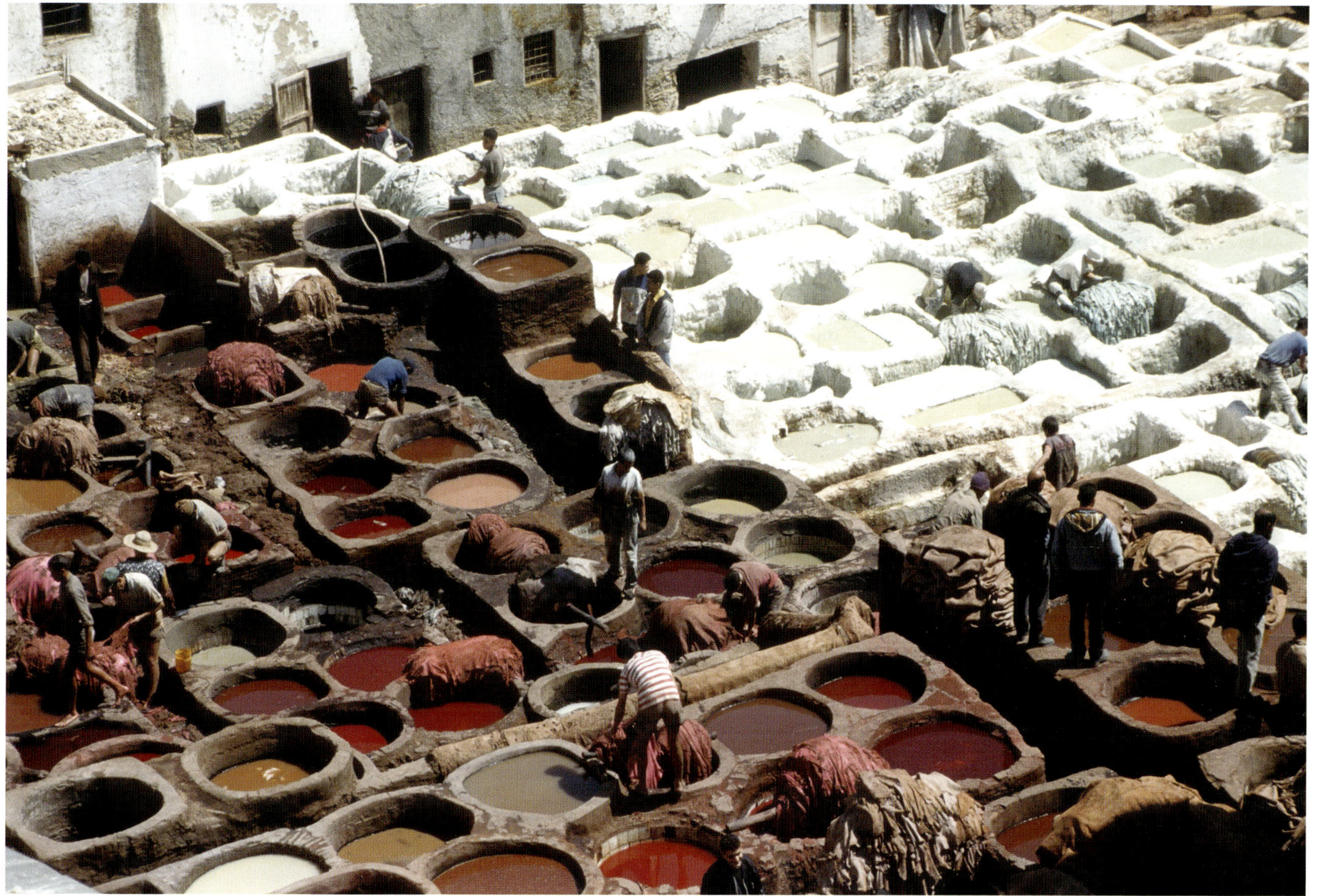

30 Tannery, Fez, Morocco

A dazzle of colours, the famous tannery in Fez is virtually unchanged since it was established here in medieval times and is a hive of activity. Circular stone vats contain thousands of animal skins which are dyed using a variety of colours. The combined odours from the skins and cow urine, which is used in the preservation of the leather, make a visit to the tanneries an unforgettable experience. The end product is top quality Moroccan leather which is highly regarded worldwide.

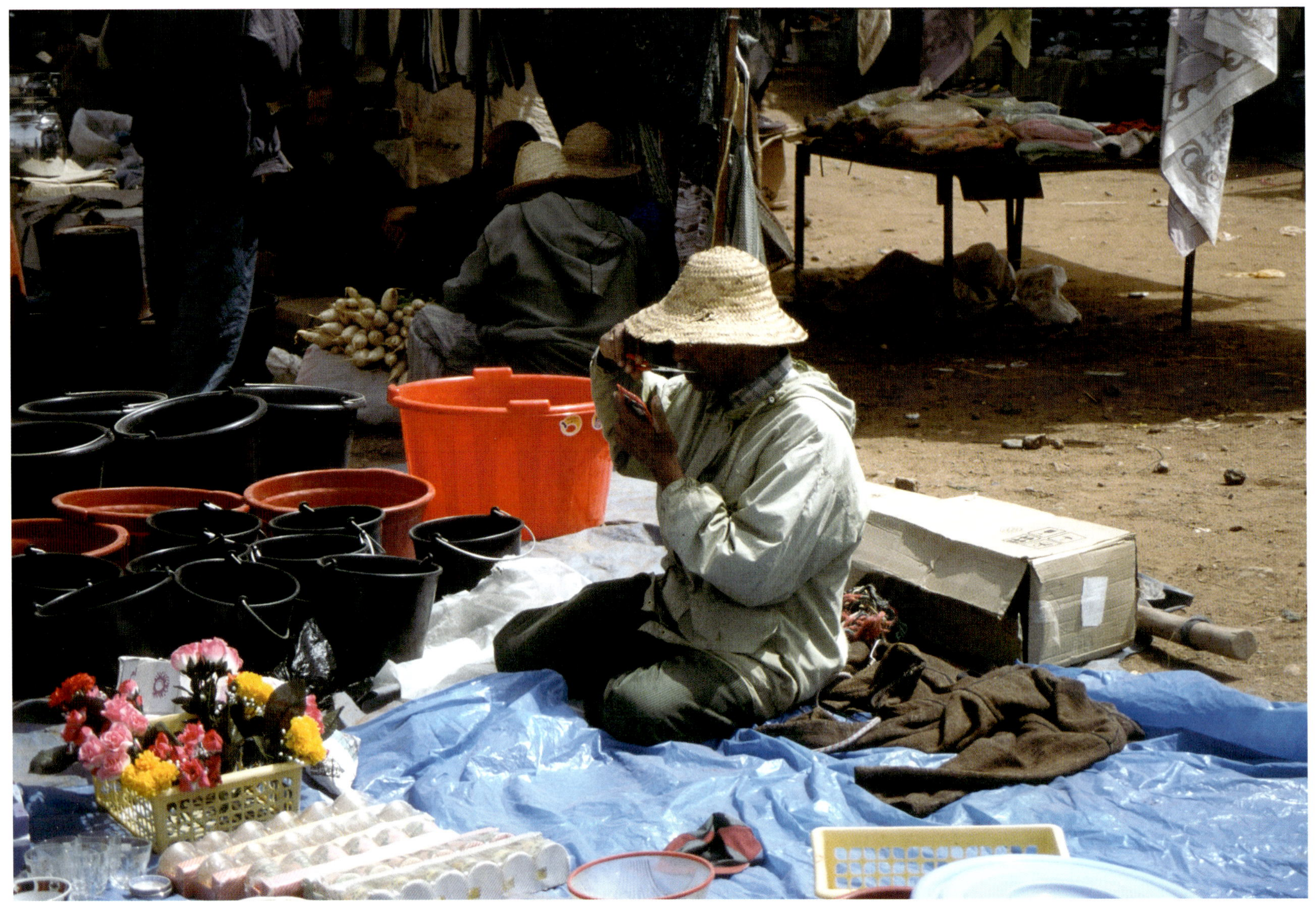

31. 'SELF-TRIM', BERBER MARKET, AMIZMIZ, ATLAS MOUNTAINS, MOROCCO

A gentleman whose business is the selling of plastic containers trims his own moustache while patiently waiting for the next customer. A visit to the weekly Berber market held at Amizmiz in the Atlas Mountains is a visual feast. Meat from freshly slaughtered cattle, sheep and goats is sold from rickety wooden stalls, bales of hay are purchased and unloaded from huge trucks, locals 'park' their donkeys in a designated holding area, itinerant smiths fix broken iron tools, freshly squeezed orange juice is proffered and the scents from an array of spices waft through the air.

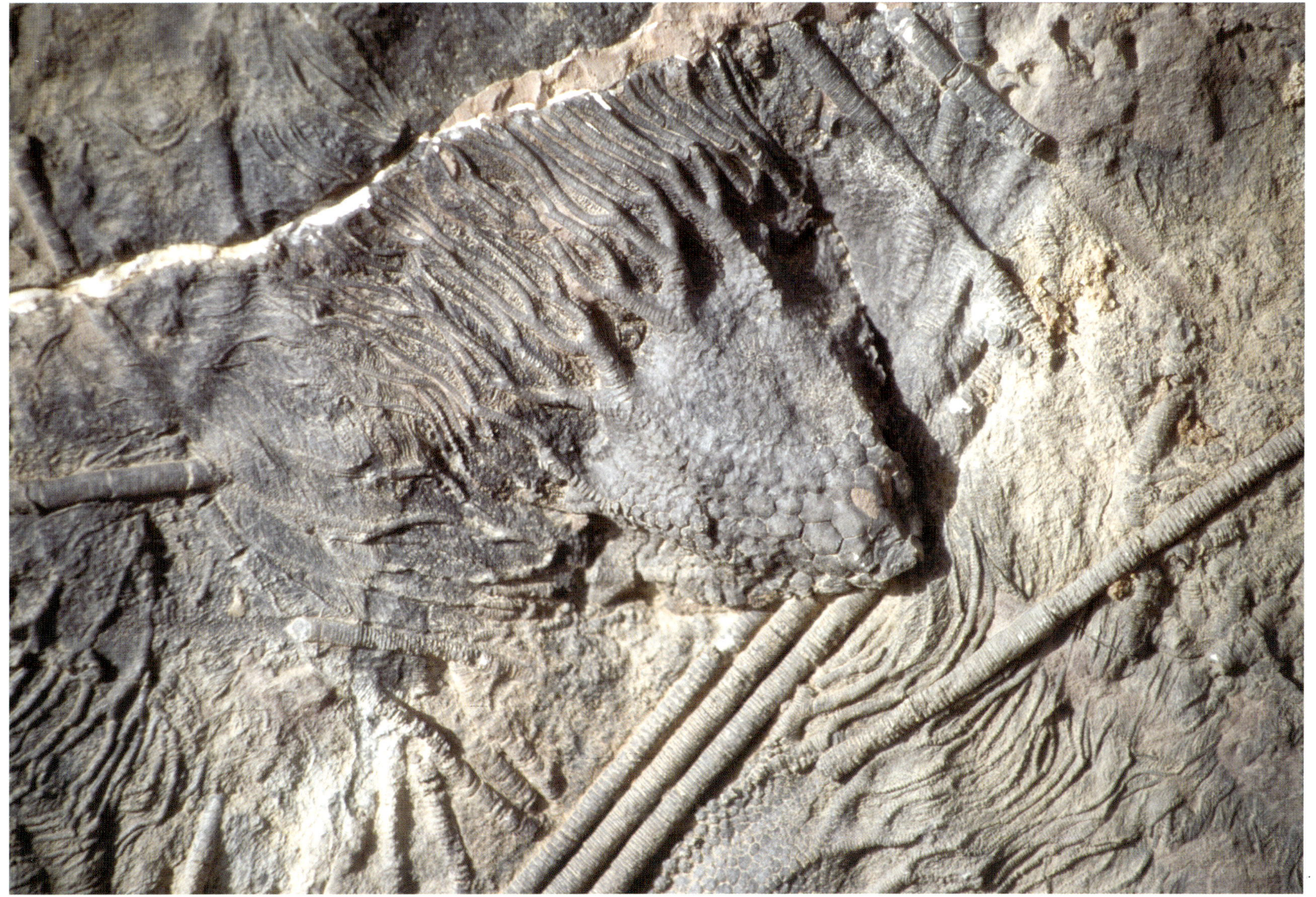

32. Fossil Sea-Lilies, Erfoud, Morocco

Although these 400 million year old crinoid fossils resemble flowers, they are in fact members of the phylum of marine animals known as echinoderms and are related to starfish and sea urchins. Also known as sea-lilies, their name derives from the Greek words 'krinon', a lily, and 'eidos' meaning 'form'. Over 6,000 fossil species have been identified. The head of the creature was equipped with a number of arms with feather-like filaments which directed food towards the mouth. It was attached to the seabed by a stalk. Many species of sea-lilies are still found today in the World's oceans.

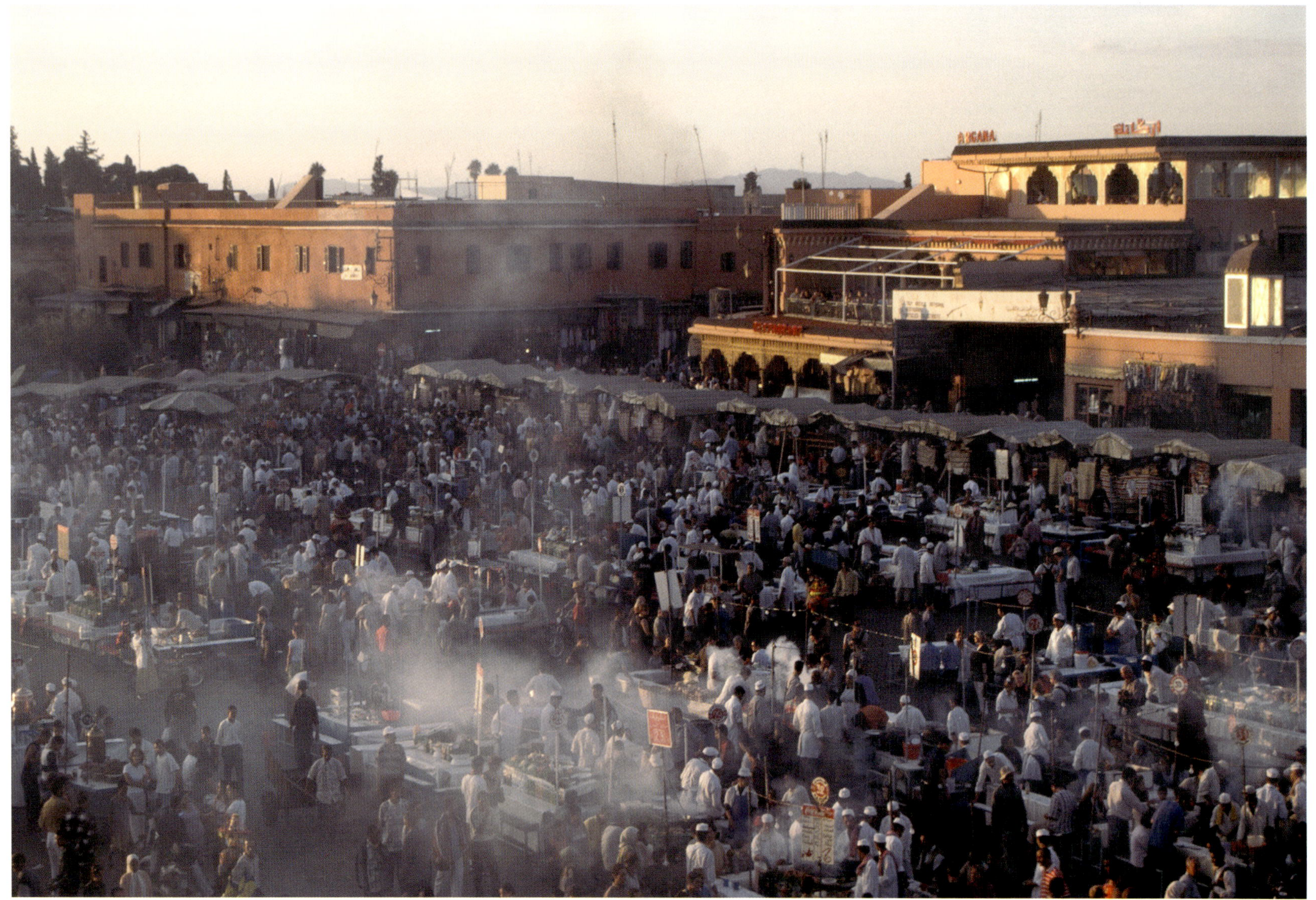

33. Djemma El Fna, Marrakesh, Morocco

Viewed to best advantage from the upstairs terrace of one of the many cafes that gird the square, the evening spectacle of Djemma el Fna is legendary. Its name means 'the meeting place of the dead' deriving from the practice in bygone days of displaying the severed heads of executed people on spikes in the square. Around 5pm every evening large numbers of street vendors set up their mobile kitchens. The scene is a babel of tongues as tourists from all over the world and locals mingle and stream between the rows of stalls. Cooked sheep brain, snails, couscous, cow tongues, goat heads and tajines are all on sale. These Moroccan style fast-food snacks can be enjoyed at adjacent tables. As the sun declines the medieval-like scene is illuminated by the vendors' gas lamps.

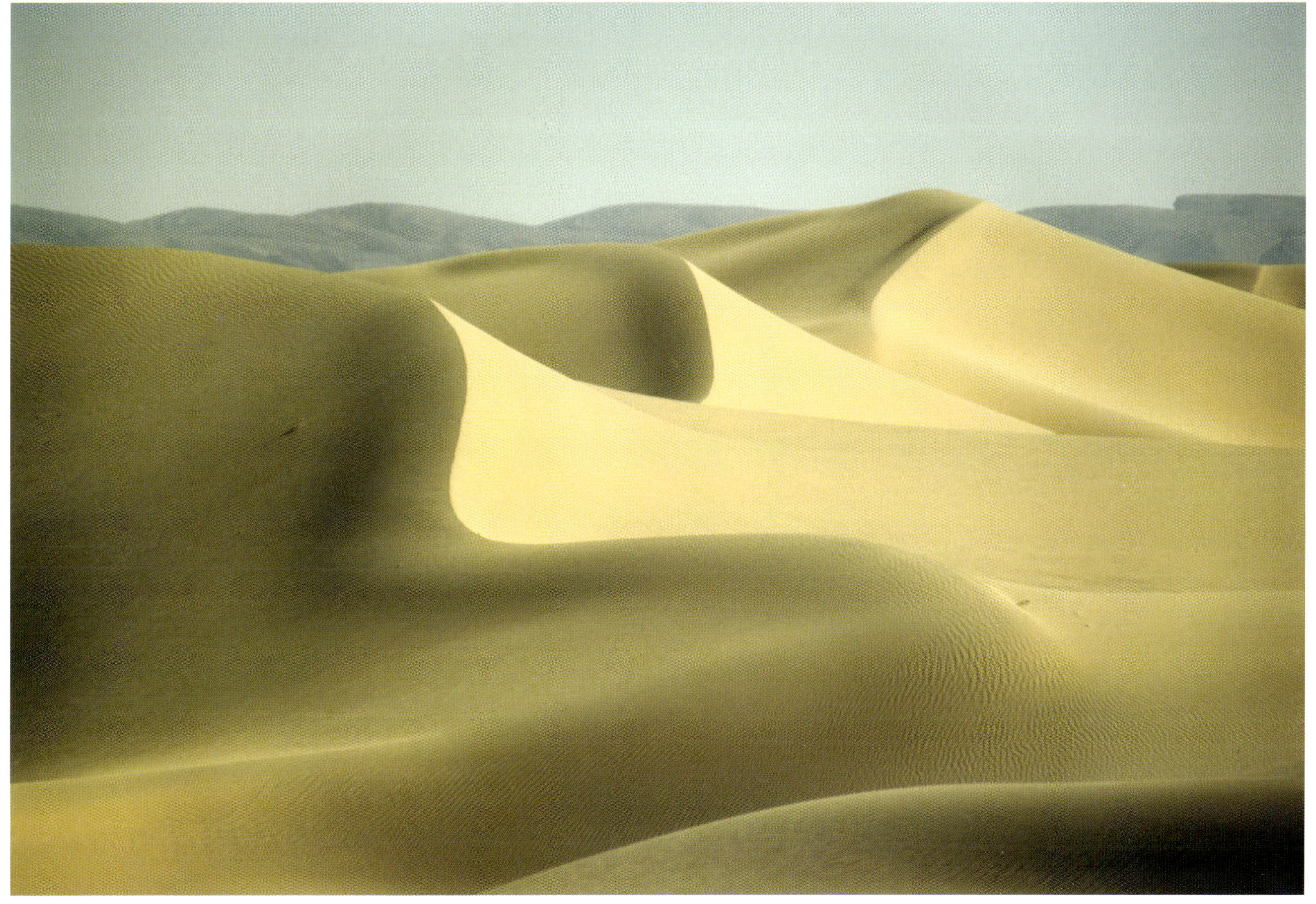

34. SAHARAN SAND DUNES, OUED MBIDIA, MOROCCO

The Sahara is the largest desert on our planet covering an approximate area of 3.5 million square miles and extends across almost the entire expanse of North Africa. Over long periods of time exposed rock is broken down as a result of diurnal temperature changes. During the day rock expands as it absorbs heat and then contracts with the fall in temperature at night. This cycle of expansion-contraction eventually reduces rock to tiny grains of sand. Moved by wind, the sand grains accumulate one by one and frequently form impressively large and extensive dune complexes, the morphology and location of which are transient.

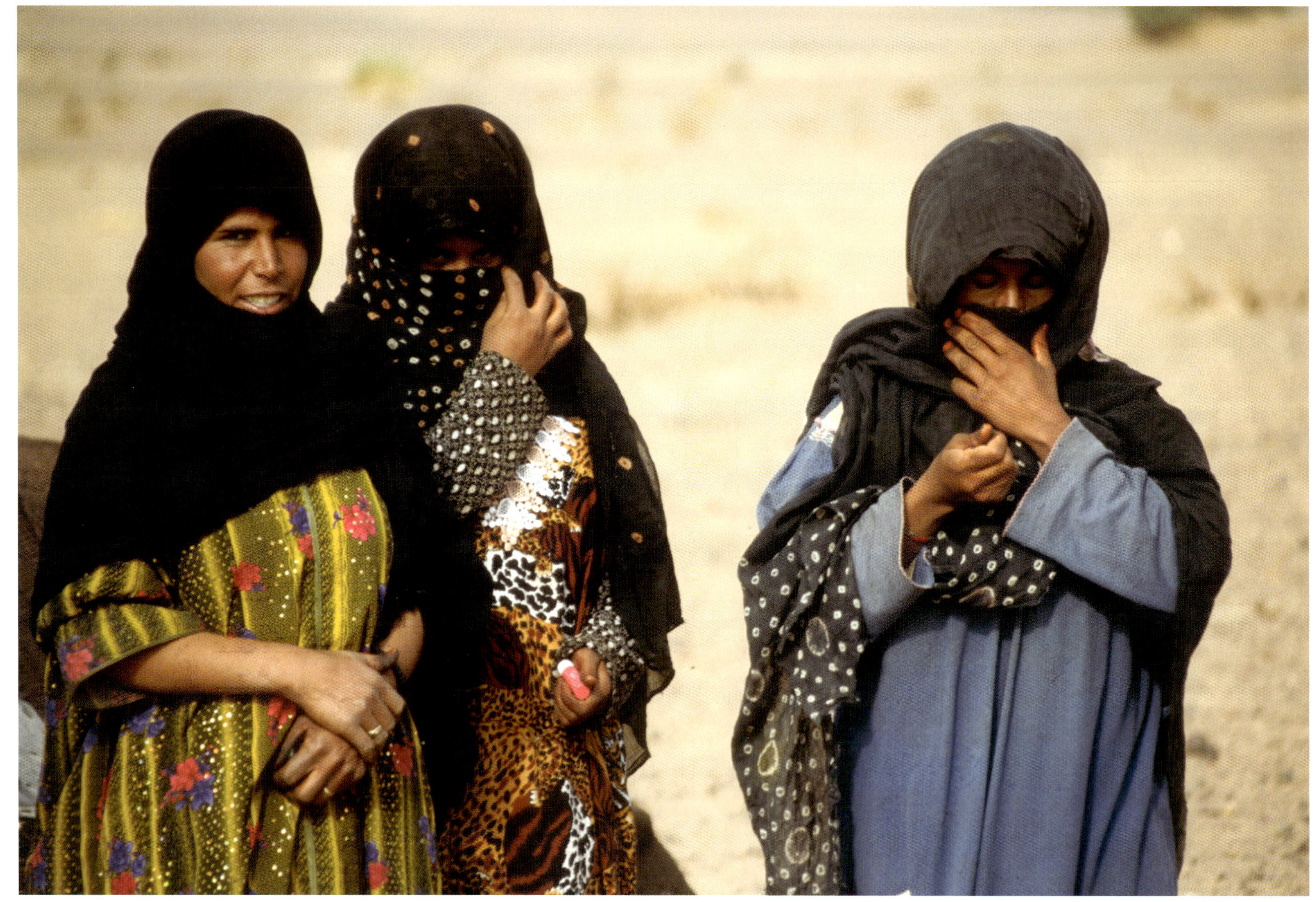

35. Berber Nomads, Bouziane, Morocco

The Berbers are the indigenous people of Morocco. Tribal based, many practice a nomadic lifestyle moving between the Atlas Mountains and Saharan desert. Menfolk tend to flocks of sheep, goats and camels while the women care for the children and older members of the family back at camp. They live in tents made from goat or camel hair. Women commonly decorate their hands with henna dye and the patterns generally last for a few weeks. Their clothing, consisting of a head covering and multi-layered, loose flowing robes, is specially designed to protect their bodies from the extreme heat of the sun.

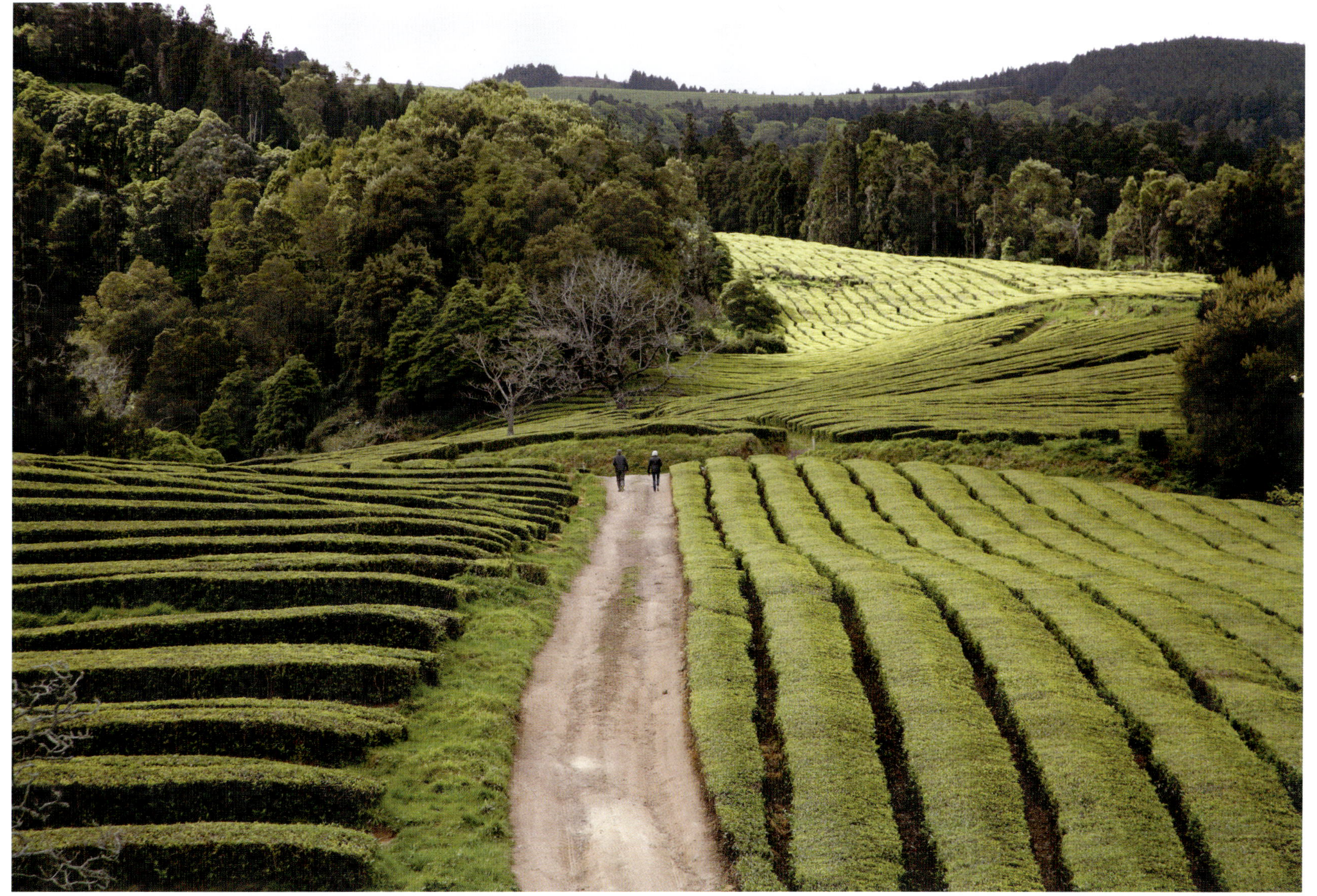

36. GORREANA TEA PLANTATION, SAO MIGUEL, AZORES, PORTUGAL

Gorreana is Europe's only tea plantation. A fifth generation family-run business, production began in 1883. The island's climate and mineral rich soils are particularly ideal for the growing of the tea plant. Gorreana's black and green teas have enjoyed an International reputation for well over a century now and are exported widely. No pesticides or other chemicals are used on the 32 acre plantation. The leaves are handpicked between April and September and around 33 tons of tea are produced annually in their small factory.

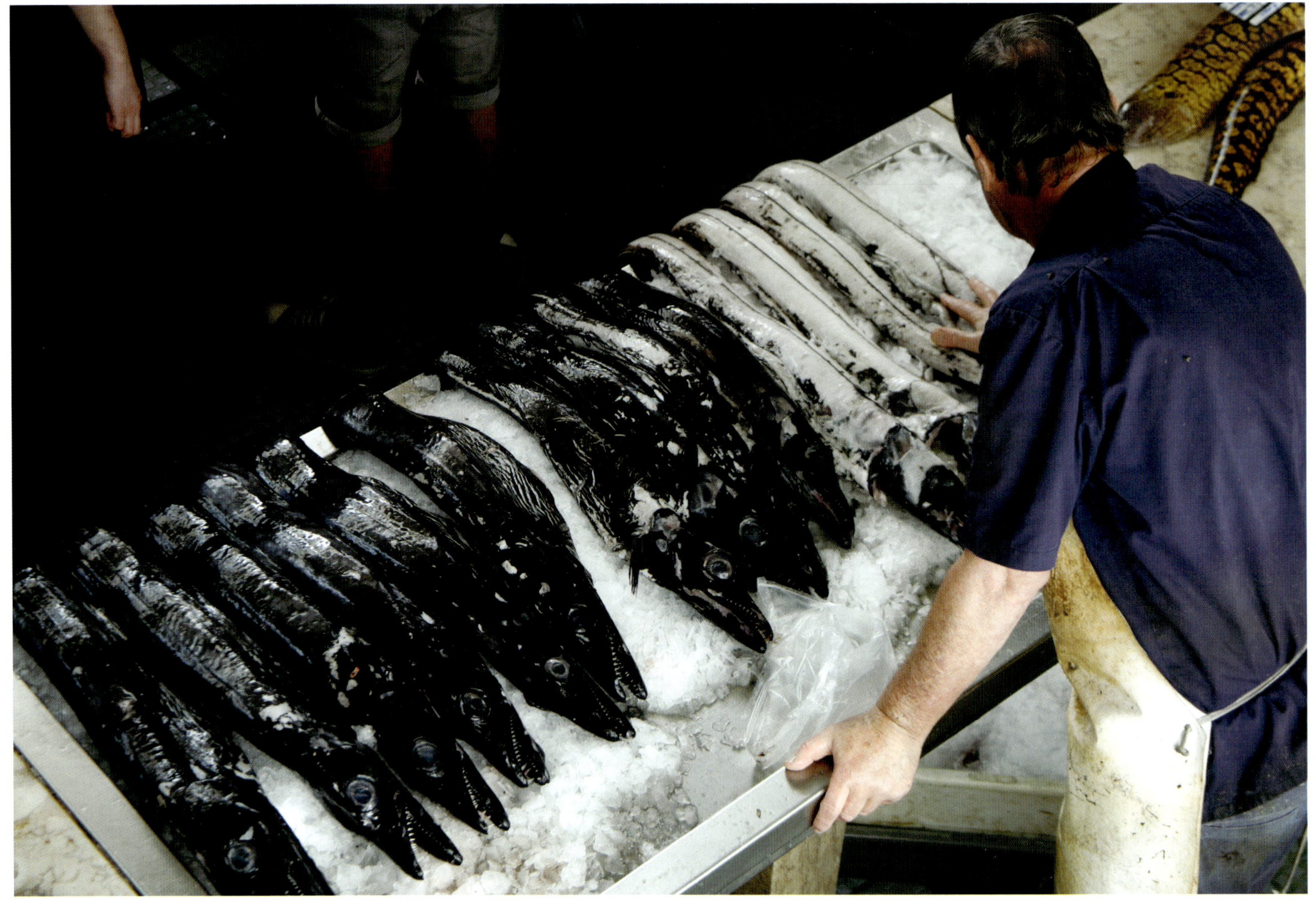

37. BLACK SCABBARD FISH, FUNCHAL, MADEIRA, PORTUGAL

A must-see for any visitor to the island of Madeira is the Mercado dos Lavradores (Farmer's Market) which was built in 1940. A local specialty sold here by the fishmongers is the black scabbard fish, *(Aphanopus carbo)*. This is a deep-water species found between 2600 and 5200 foot below the surface. A highly efficient predator, it has formidable needle-sharp teeth. Its eel-like body can be over 6 feet long. Local fishermen from the picturesque town of Camara de Lobos use specialized baited lines, that can be over a mile in length, to catch large quantities of the fish.

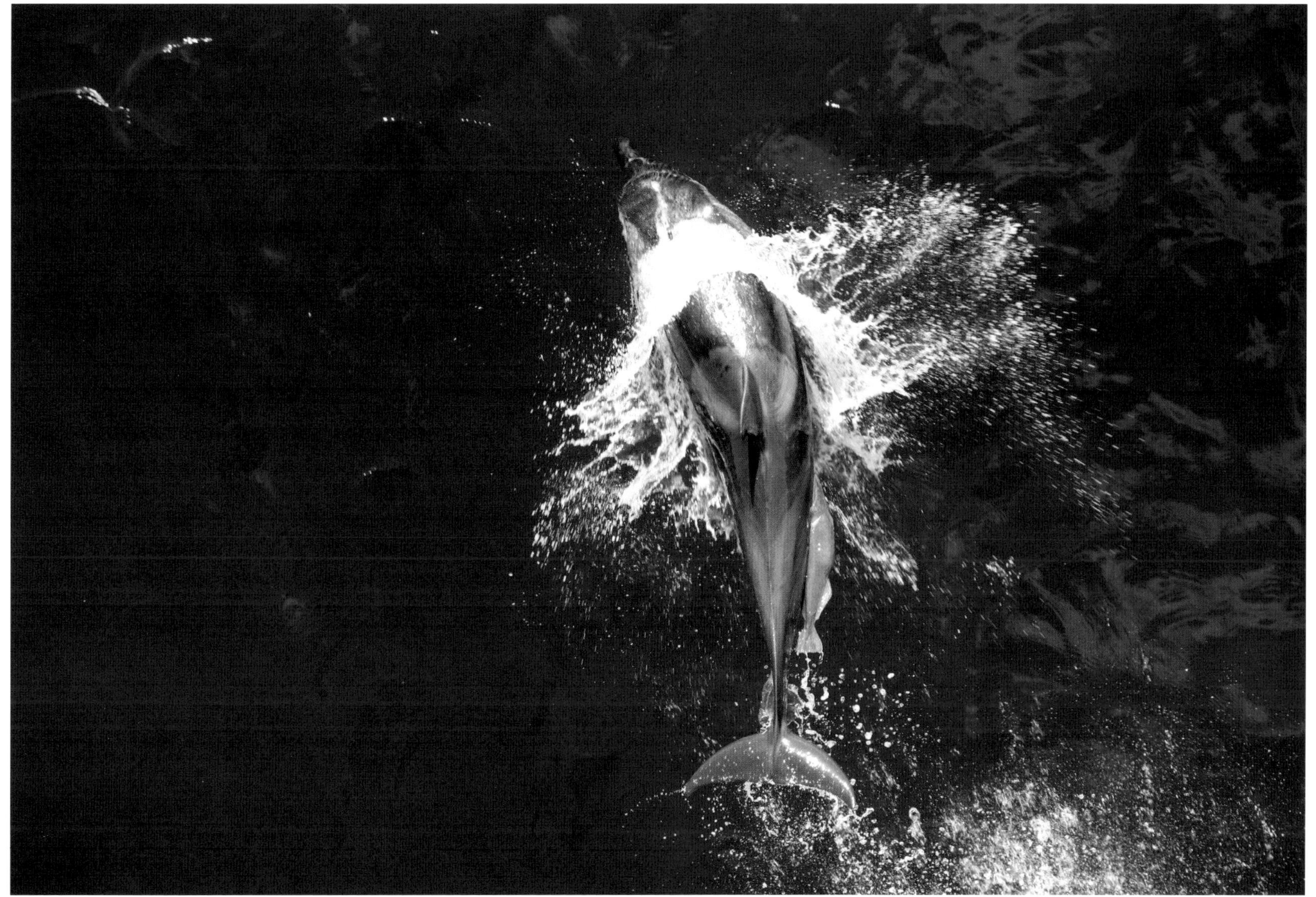

38. Striped Dolphin and Remora, La Gomera, Canary Islands, Spain

The striped dolphin *(Stenella coeruleoalba)* often displays its acrobatic skills with somersaults and tailspins while bow riding ships, like this one off the coast of La Gomera in the Canary Islands. Reaching an average length of 8 feet, an adult weighs between 14 and 24 stone. Their diet mainly consists of fish and squid which they hunt down to a depth of 650 feet. Groups of between 100 and 500 dolphins are common but occasionally large schools of 3,000 or more have been observed. A remora is attached to its right flank. These warm water fish affix themselves to large fish, sharks and dolphins by a specialized oval sucking disc on its long flattened head. Hitching a free ride, remoras feed on scraps from the host's meals. They are pelagic fish living in the open sea.

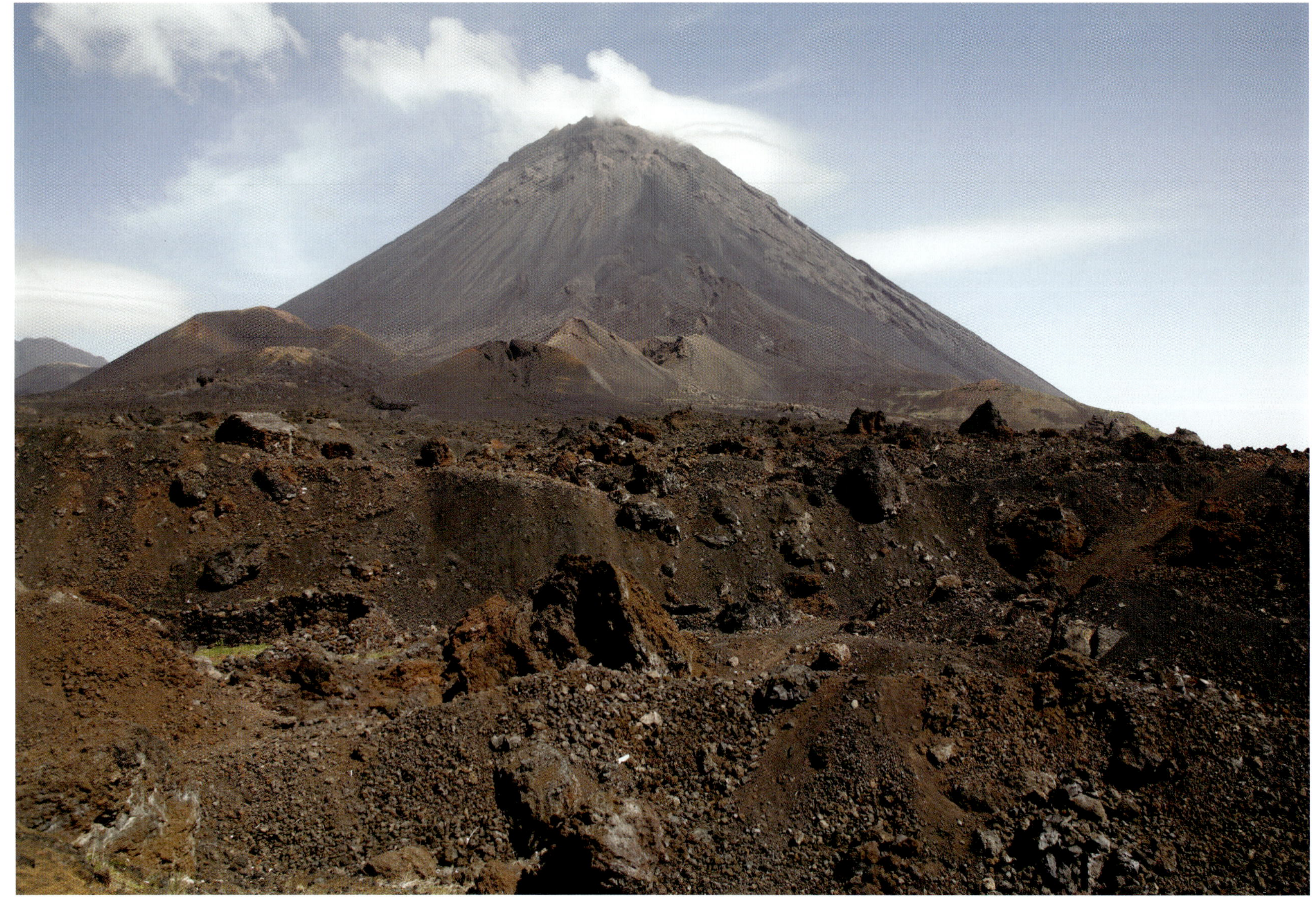

39. Pico Do Fogo, Fogo Island, Cape Verde Islands

The volcanic islands of Cape Verde lie 400 miles off Senegal in West Africa and were settled by the Portuguese in the 15th century. The island of Fogo is still sporadically active. Pico de Fogo is the main cone of a massive volcano system and rises over 9,200 feet above a 5 and a half mile wide caldera. Its volcanic soils support a small wine industry. An eruption began on its flank on 23 November 2014. Thousands of local people were forced to evacuate their homes and a number of villages were completely destroyed by subsequent lava flows. Only six weeks earlier, myself and 60 other guests and staff on a trip aboard the *National Geographic Explorer* had enjoyed a delicious lunch in a small restaurant in one of those villages.

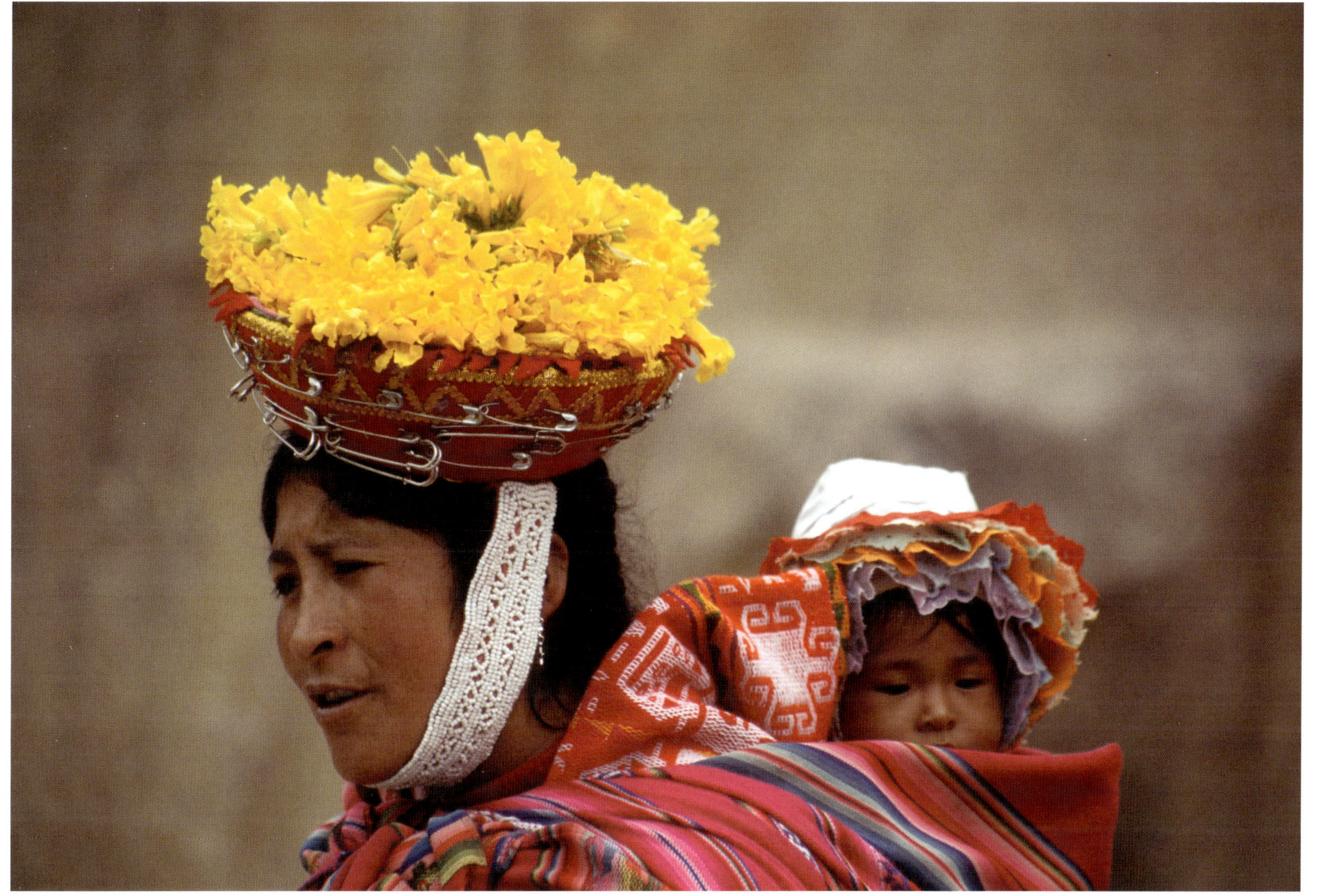

40. SOUVENIR SELLER, OLLANTAYTAMBO, PERU

A local Quechua woman with her child safely enveloped in a wraparound on her back sells souvenir trinkets among the ruins of the once great Inca fortress at Ollantaytambo. This was one of the most important centres of Inca military power and dominated the northern end of the Sacred Valley. She lives in one of the centuries-old houses in the town that has changed little since the arrival of the Spanish Conquistadors. Here she raises guinea pigs, an Andean delicacy, which are kept in sizable numbers in her kitchen. These will be roasted, fried or stewed.

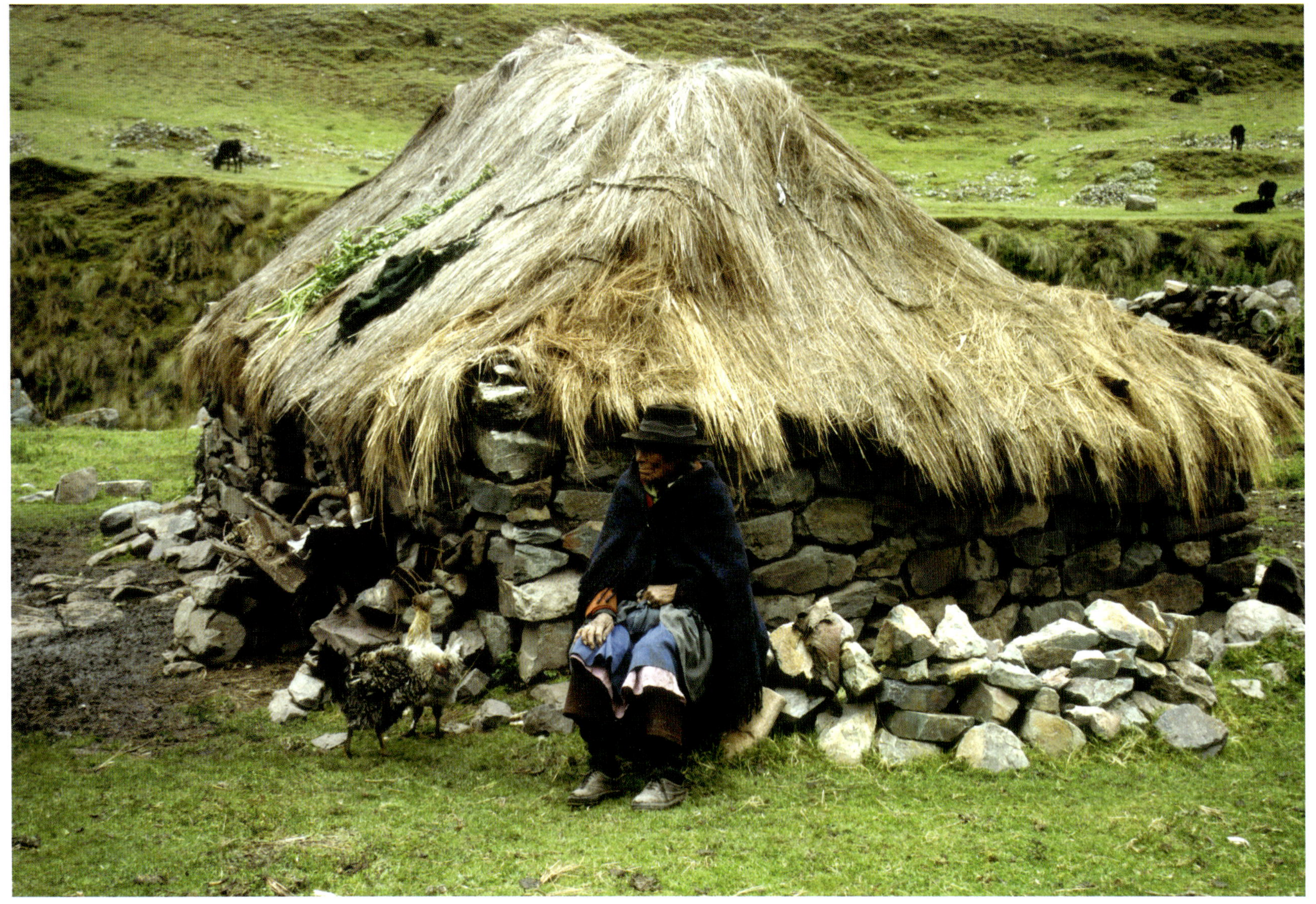

41. Traditional Andean Home, Angascocha, Peru

An elderly woman relaxes outside her house high up in the Peruvian Andes. Comparable in many ways to an Irish traditional cottage, the house is completely fashioned from materials sourced locally. The gaps between the individual blocks of stone in the walls are packed with clay to help reduce drafts. Windows are absent, as is a chimney, the smoke from the fire inside filtering directly through the rudimentary 'thatch' which is anchored by ropes to a frame of roof timbers underneath. Hens supply eggs and fresh milk and meat are provided by a small herd of goats.

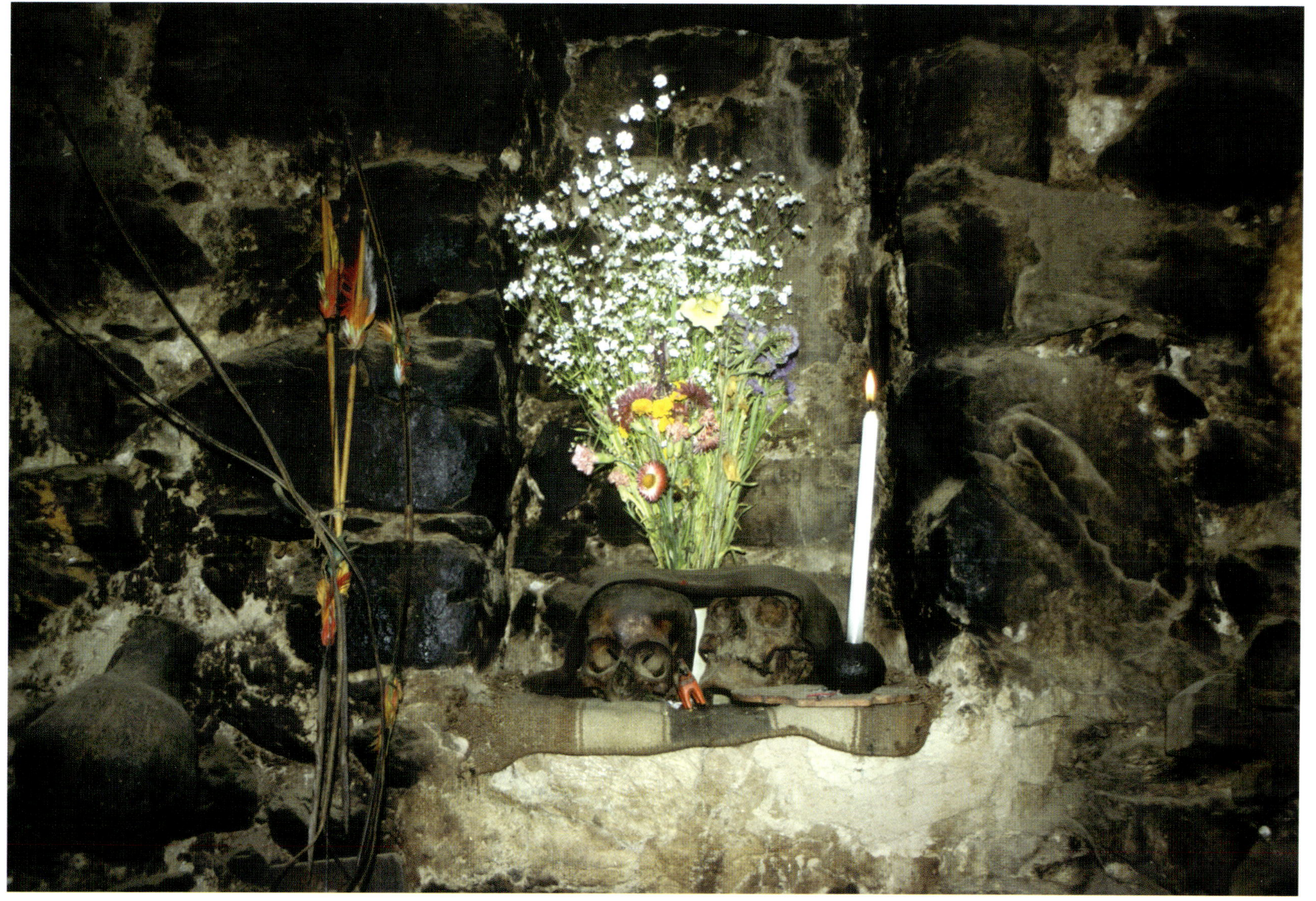

42. ANCESTOR SHRINE, OLLANTAYTAMBO, PERU

Ancestor worship is a ritual found in many cultures worldwide and takes on a multiplicity of expression. In this house in Ollantaytamb, the skulls of grandparents are the centerpieces of a small shrine centrally placed in a special niche above the fireplace. It is held that the departed keep watch over the members of the family living in the home, guarding against misfortune and hardship. Adorned with bouquets of flowers and lighted candles, these shrines are somewhat comparable to May Altars, a once common feature in Irish homes.

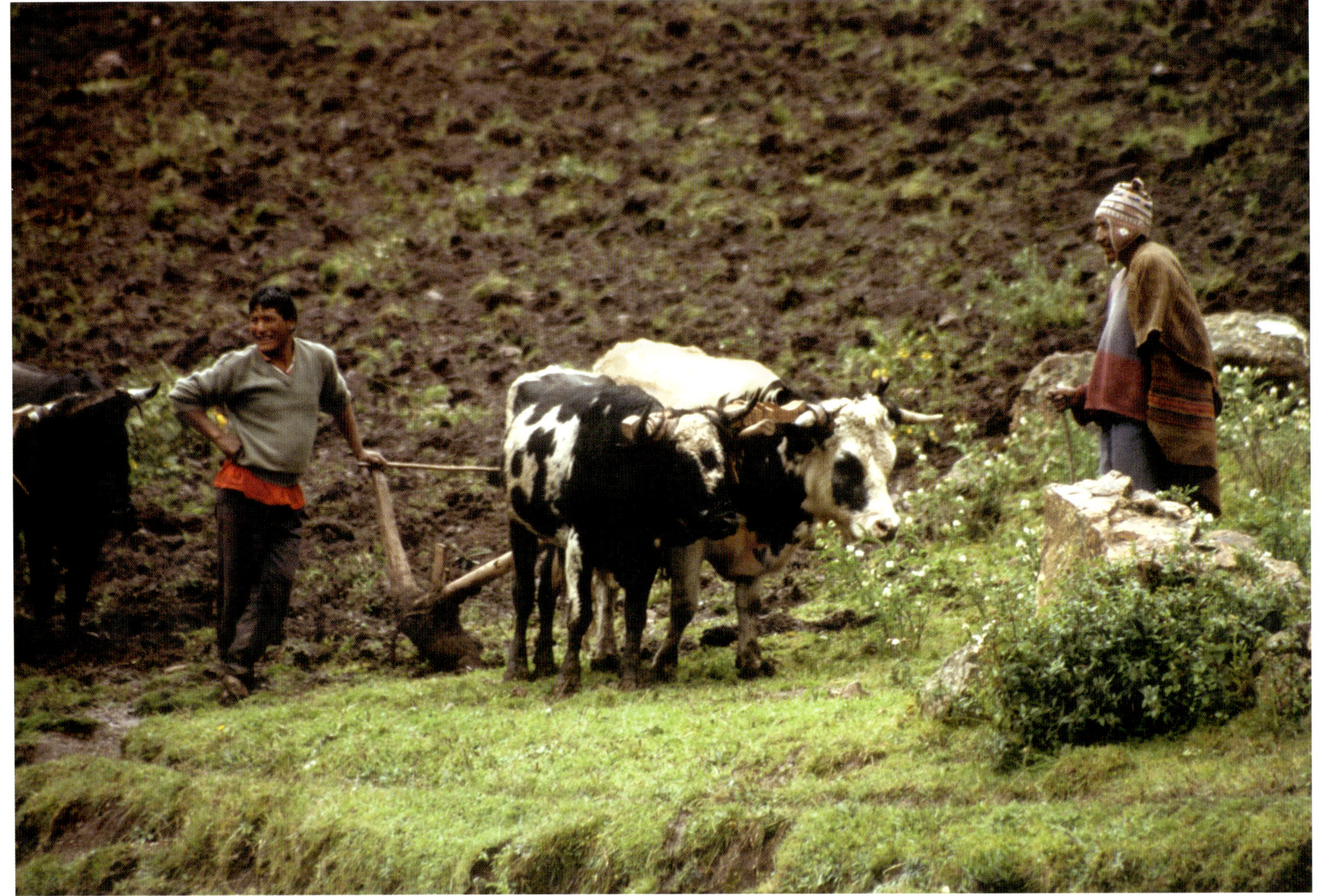

43. PLOUGHING WITH OXEN, SOQMA, PERU

Taking a short break to exchange a few words, this farmer in the Peruvian Andes leans on his ox-drawn wooden plough in a scene not much changed over the centuries. When ploughing is underway, his friend will assist by leading the oxen along the steeply inclined valley side by a rope attached to the wooden yoke. Working these heavy, damp upland soils is a difficult task. A wide variety of crops are cultivated in these high valleys, including potatoes, maize, beans and vegetables.

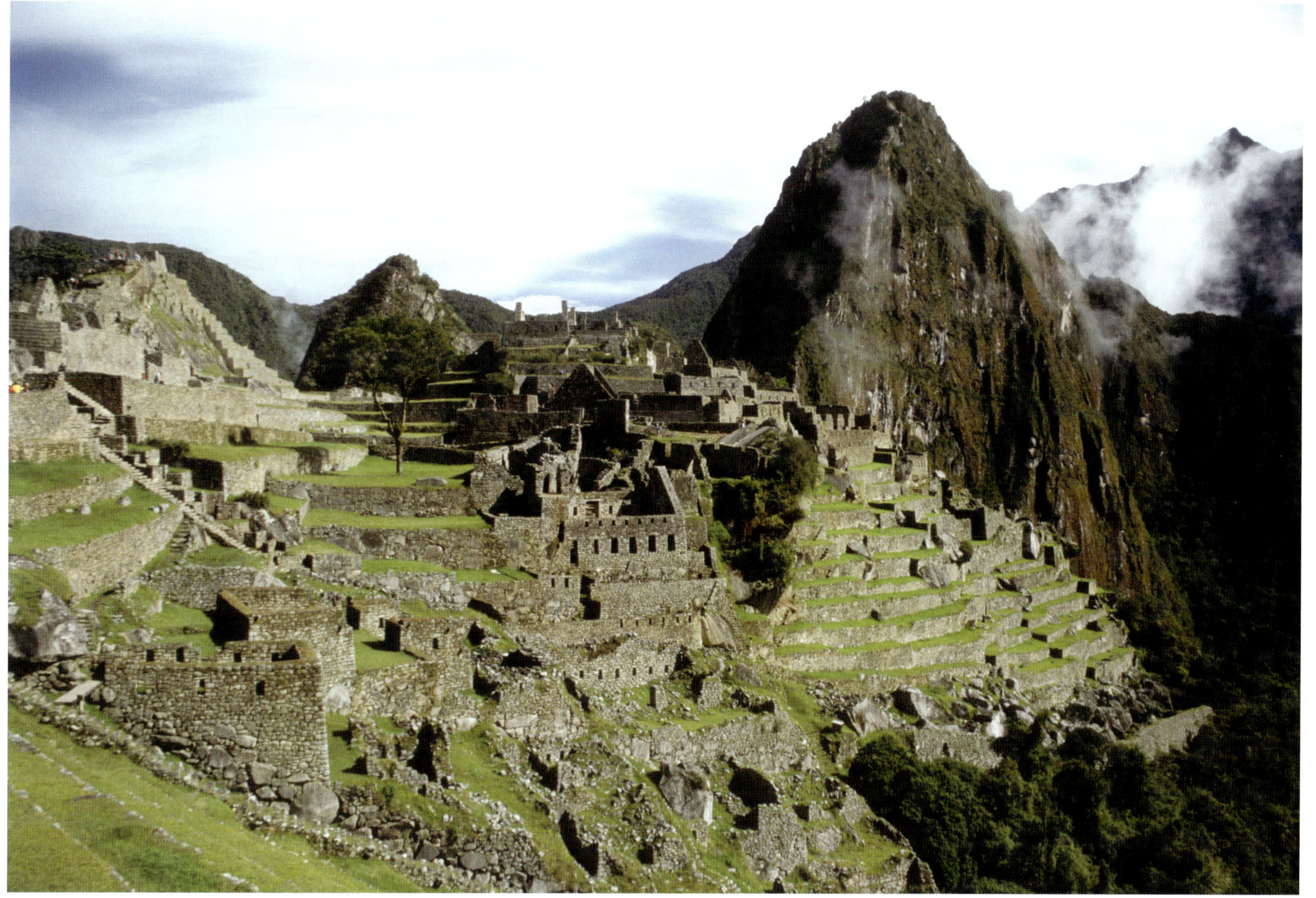

44. Machu Picchu, Peru

Set between two peaks on a 8,800 foot high mountain saddle, Machu Picchu ('Old Peak') is the most iconic of Peru's ancient Inca sites. In 1911 a scholar from Yale University, Hiram Bingham, discovered the ruins of this once thriving Inca centre hidden by forest vegetation. The complex consists of the remains of 200 dwellings and numerous temples, altars and fountains. Crops were grown on an extensive area of stone-faced cultivation terraces which had been watered by an elaborate irrigation system. The remarkable civilization of the Incas was brought to an abrupt and bloody end in 1532 by Francisco Pizarro and his Spanish Conquistadors.

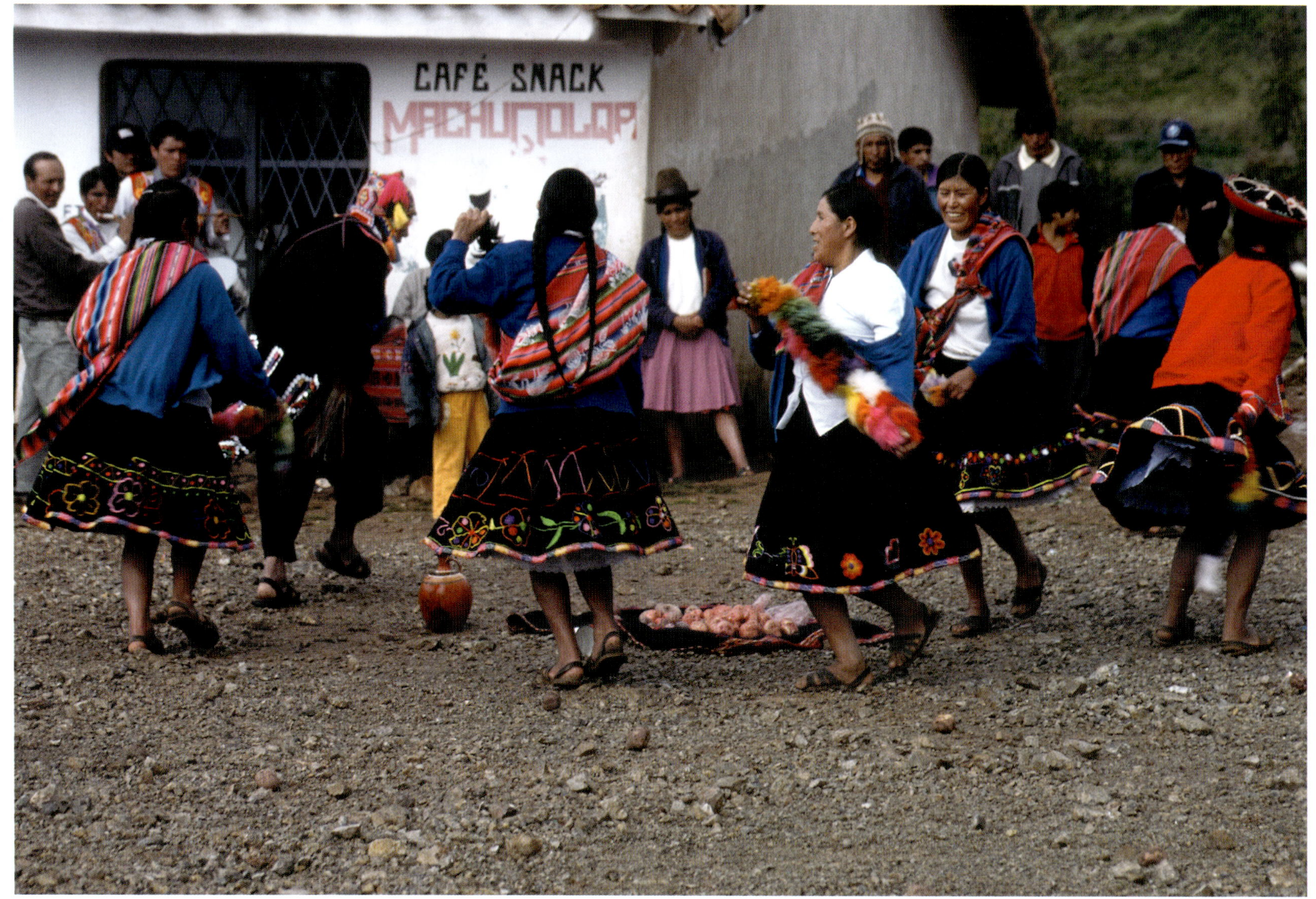

45. Potato Celebration, Cachicata, Peru

Attired in traditional dress, a man and a group of women in a village high on the flank of the Sacred Valley in Peru dance around potatoes placed on a small blanket on the ground while crowds of their fellows gather to watch. They have come together to celebrate a successful potato harvest, an event known as the 'First Tuber' ceremony. This is one of a number of similar festival get-togethers replicated throughout Peru, which punctuate the agricultural year. Archaeological research has indicated that potatoes had been domesticated by Andean peoples 8,000 years ago. Highly nutritious and prolific, the potato is a mainstay of Peruvian cuisine.

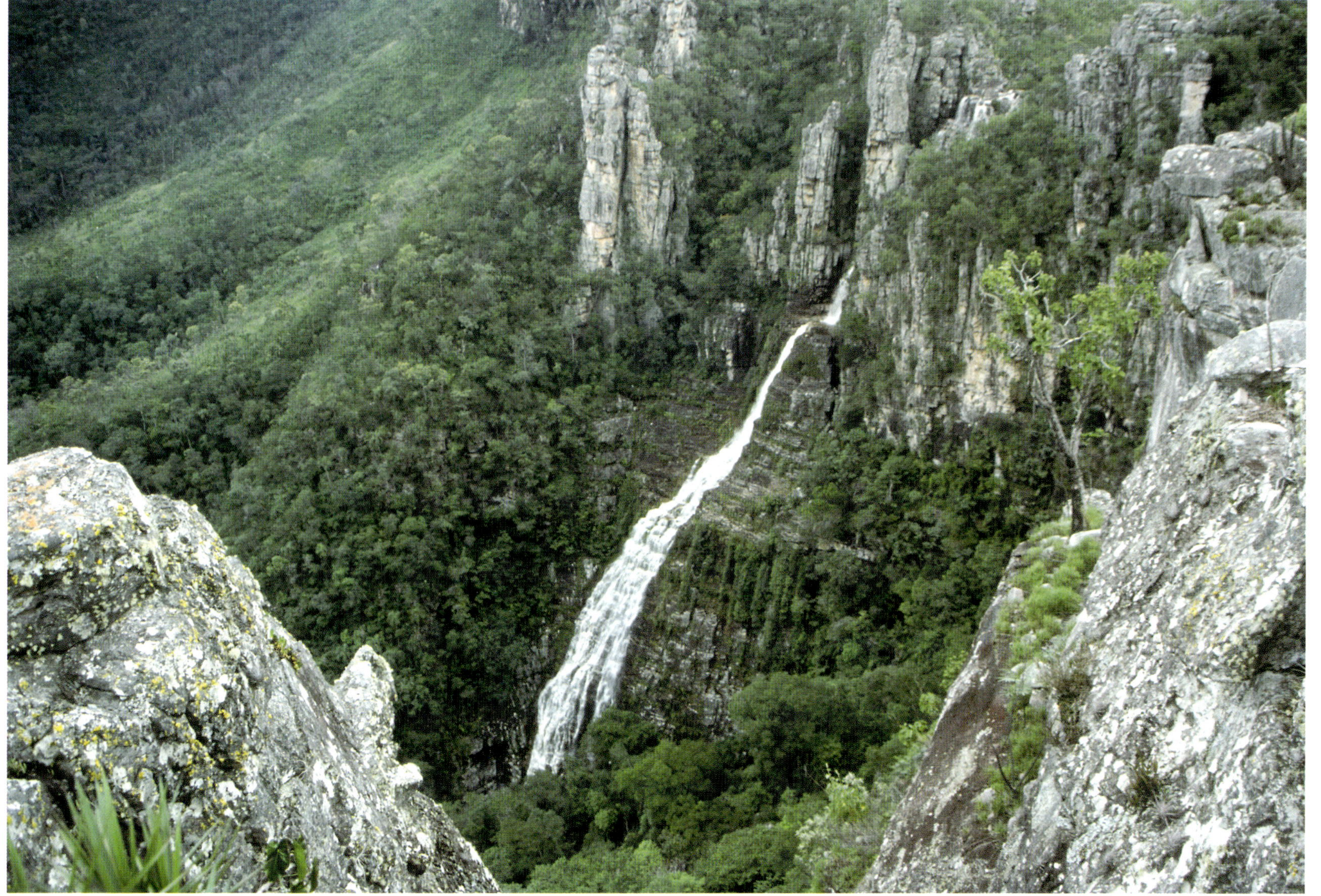

46. Chapada Dos Veadeiros National Park, Goiás, Brazil

A river cascades down the flank of an extensive plateau in the Chapada dos Veadeiros National Park, in the state of Goiás. The rock here is estimated to be in the region of 1.8 billion years old. The park was opened in 1961 and covers an area of over 250 square miles. Consisting predominantly of savanna vegetation, it has a remarkably rich biodiversity of international importance. Toucans, parakeets and macaws are glimpsed as transient splashes of colour that are all too quickly lost in the tangled verdant canvas of the forest.

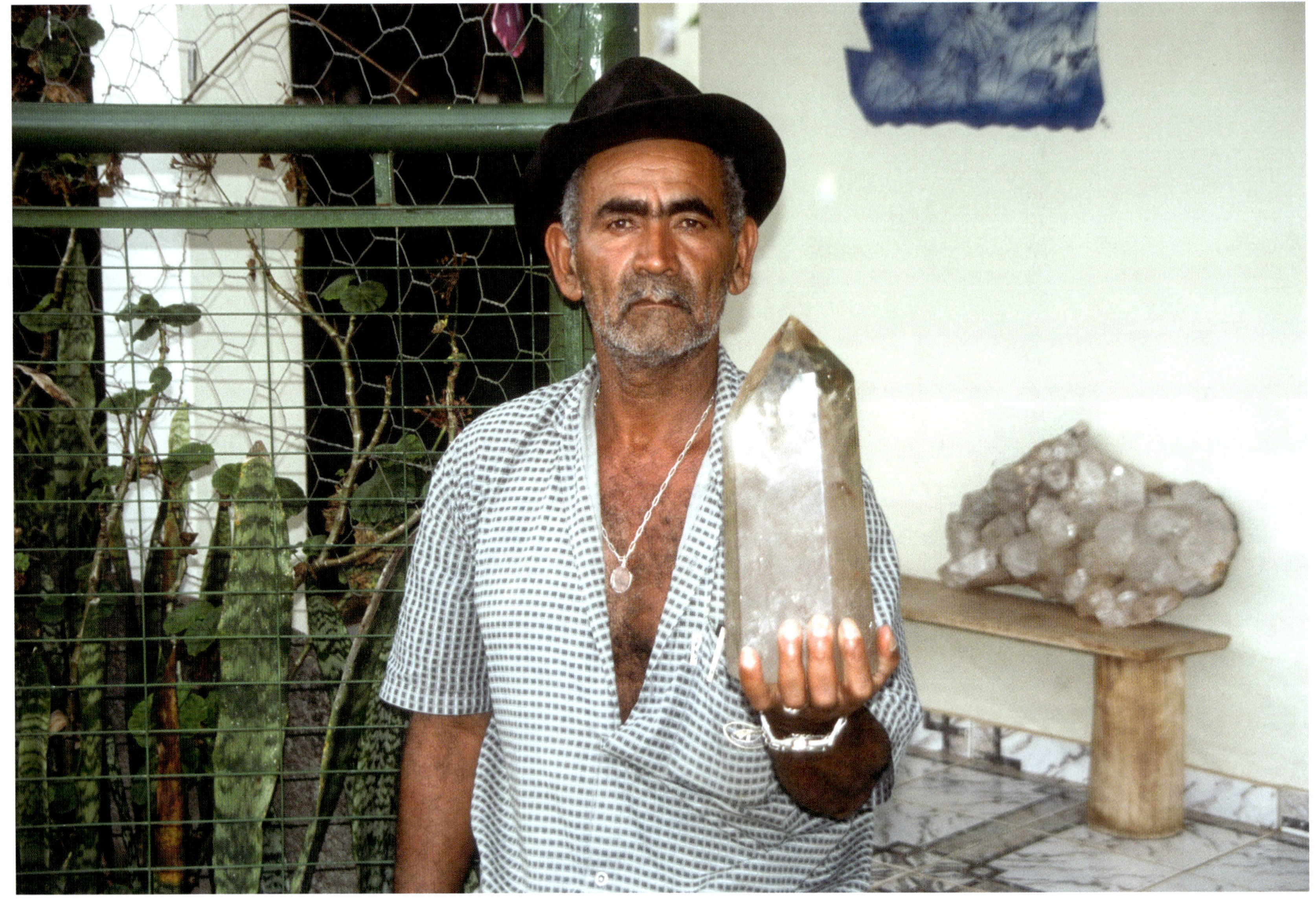

47. Crystal Seller, Alto Paraíso De Goiás, Brazil

A retired quartz miner proudly exhibits a large crystal outside his shop in Alto Paraíso. Brazil is internationally famous for the range and quality of its minerals and crystals. During the Second World War most of the quartz crystal that was used in the manufacturing of Allied radios was mined there. Quartz is a very common mineral and occurs in a variety of colours including purple, pink and yellow. The purest is colourless and is known as rock crystal. The modern resurgence in belief in the supposed beneficial and curative power inherent in crystals has boosted the trade in Brazilian minerals.

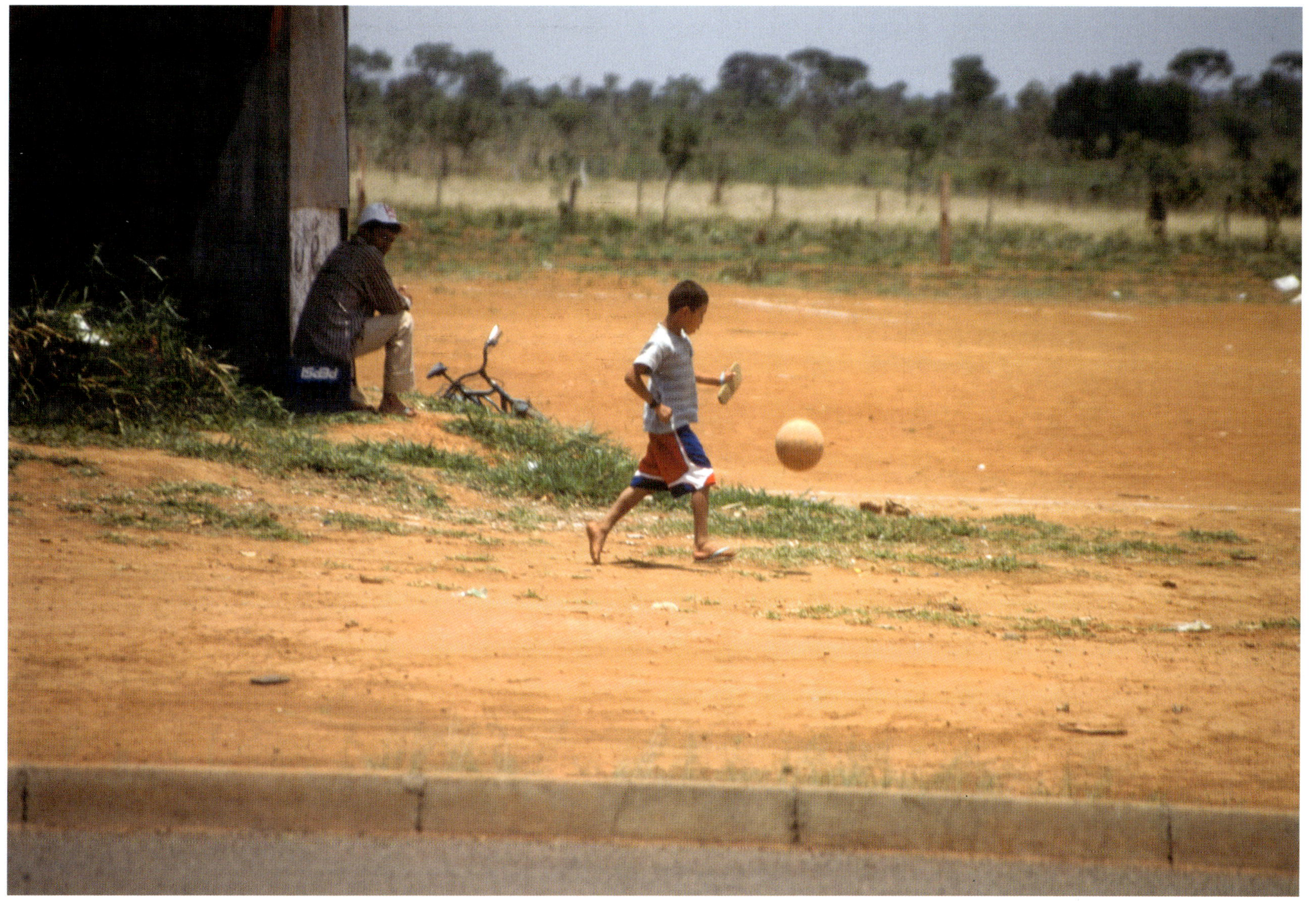

48. 'THE WORLD AT HIS FEET', SAO JORGE, BRAZIL

A young boy heads out toward a grassless pitch to play soccer, just as Edson Arantes do Nascimento probably did as a youth. Better known as Pelé, he first came to international attention in 1958 when he played on the National Brazilian team in Sweden during the World Cup. He was only 17 when he scored two of the five goals that secured a win in the final against the host country. He is widely regarded as the greatest footballer of all time.

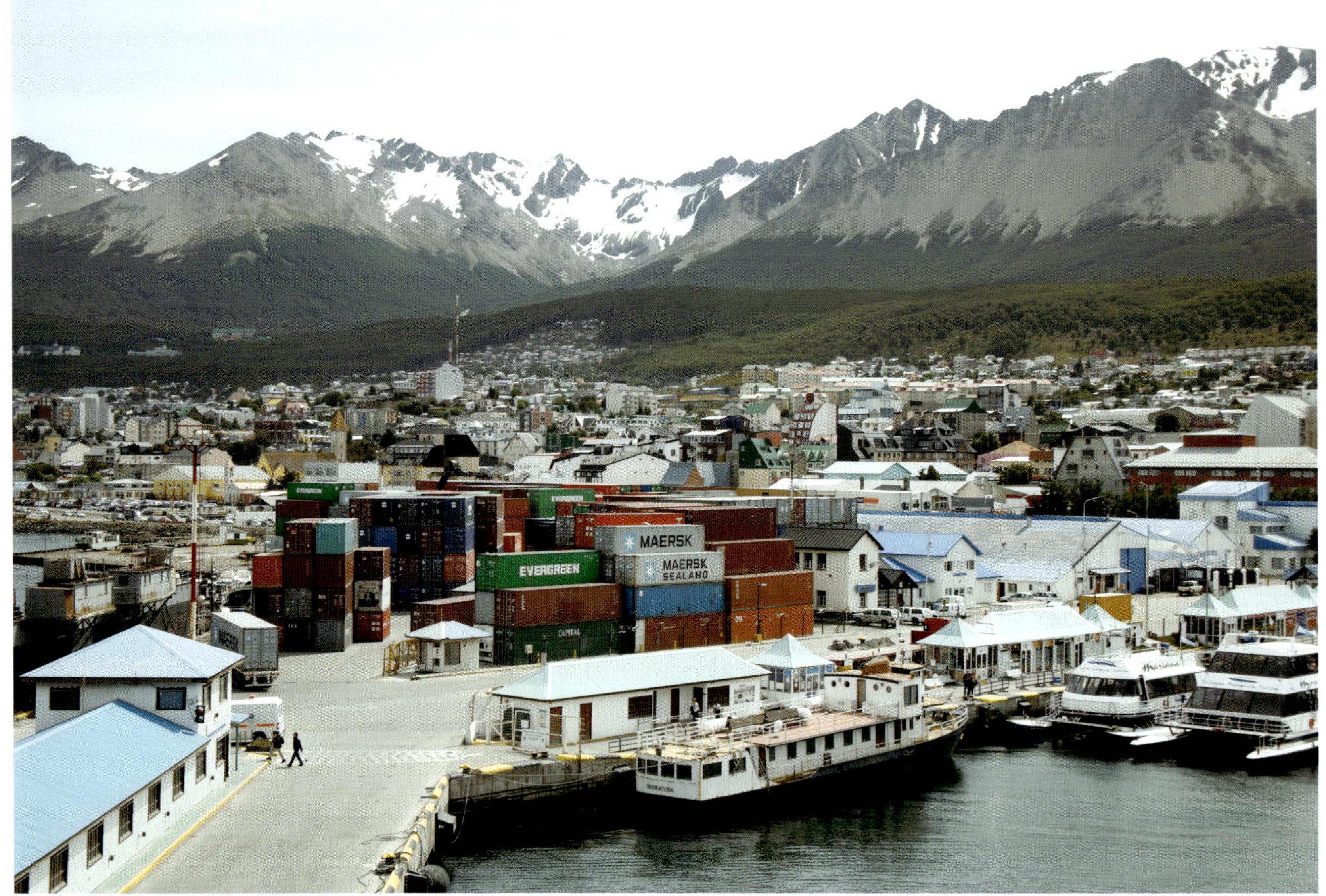

49. Ushuaia, Tierra Del Fuego, Argentina

Nestled at the foot of the Martial Mountains, Ushuaia is reputed to be the southernmost city in the world and even boasts an 'Irish Bar'. On the island of Tierra del Fuego, Ushuaia is the gateway to Antarctica via the Beagle Channel, named after a British Naval survey ship that visited here in 1832. Onboard was a twenty-two year old named Charles Darwin. It was during this five-year-long voyage that the young naturalist, known fondly by his fellow shipmates as 'the flycatcher', began to formulate his theory of evolution.

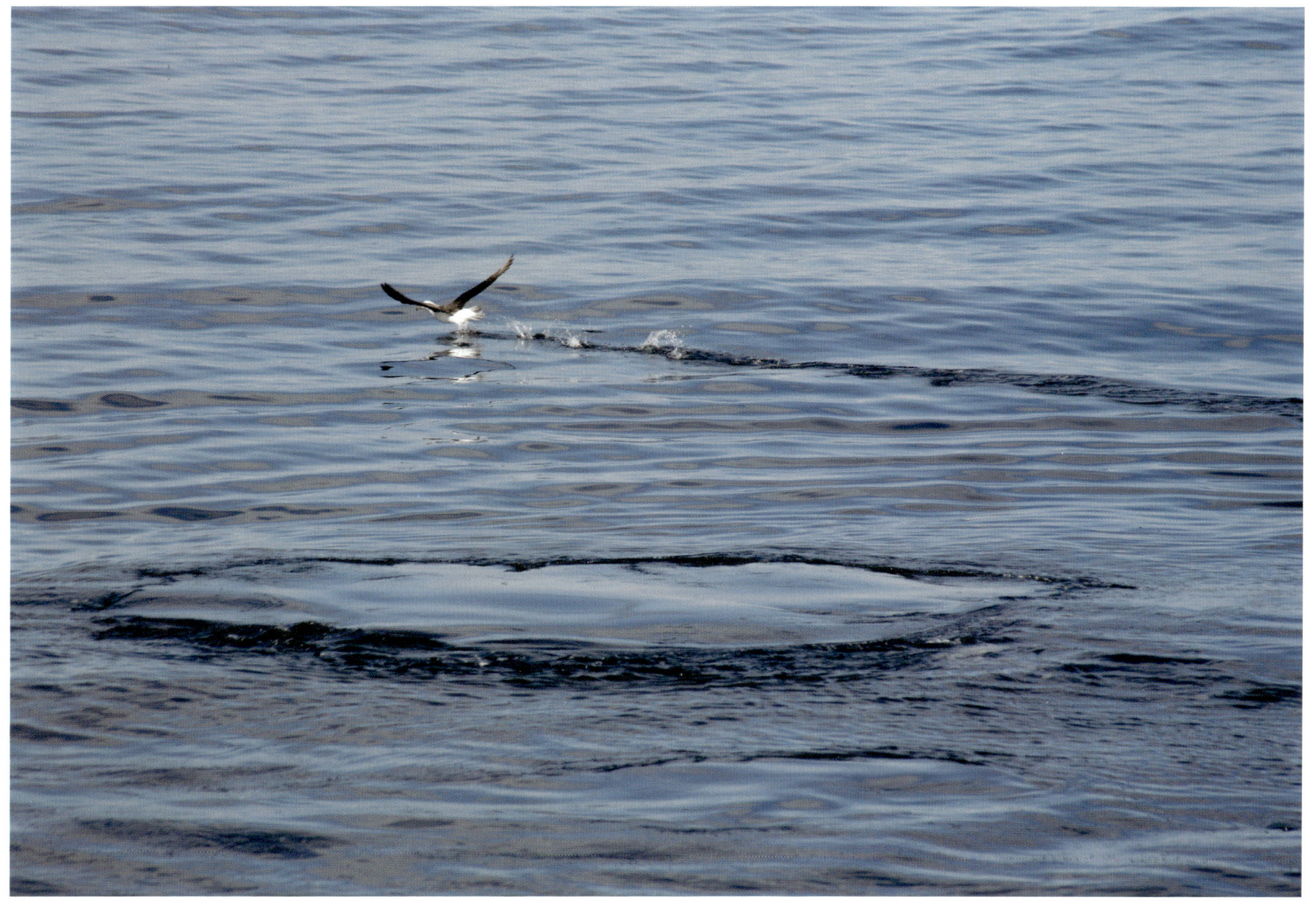

50. SEI WHALE 'FOOTPRINT' AND BLACK- BROWED ALBATROSS, BEAGLE CHANNEL, TIERRA DEL FUEGO, ARGENTINA

When a whale dives the downward stroke of its flukes creates a patch of disturbed water on the surface known as a 'whale footprint'. The sei is a baleen whale that feeds on planktonic crustaceans, squid and small fish which it skims from the water. In the South Atlantic its main food is krill. An average adult is around 50 feet in length and weighs in at between 20 and 30 tons. The black-browed is one of the smallest and the most widespread member of the albatross family. It eats crustaceans, fish, squid and carrion. Oil is produced in their stomachs which they spit at potential attackers.

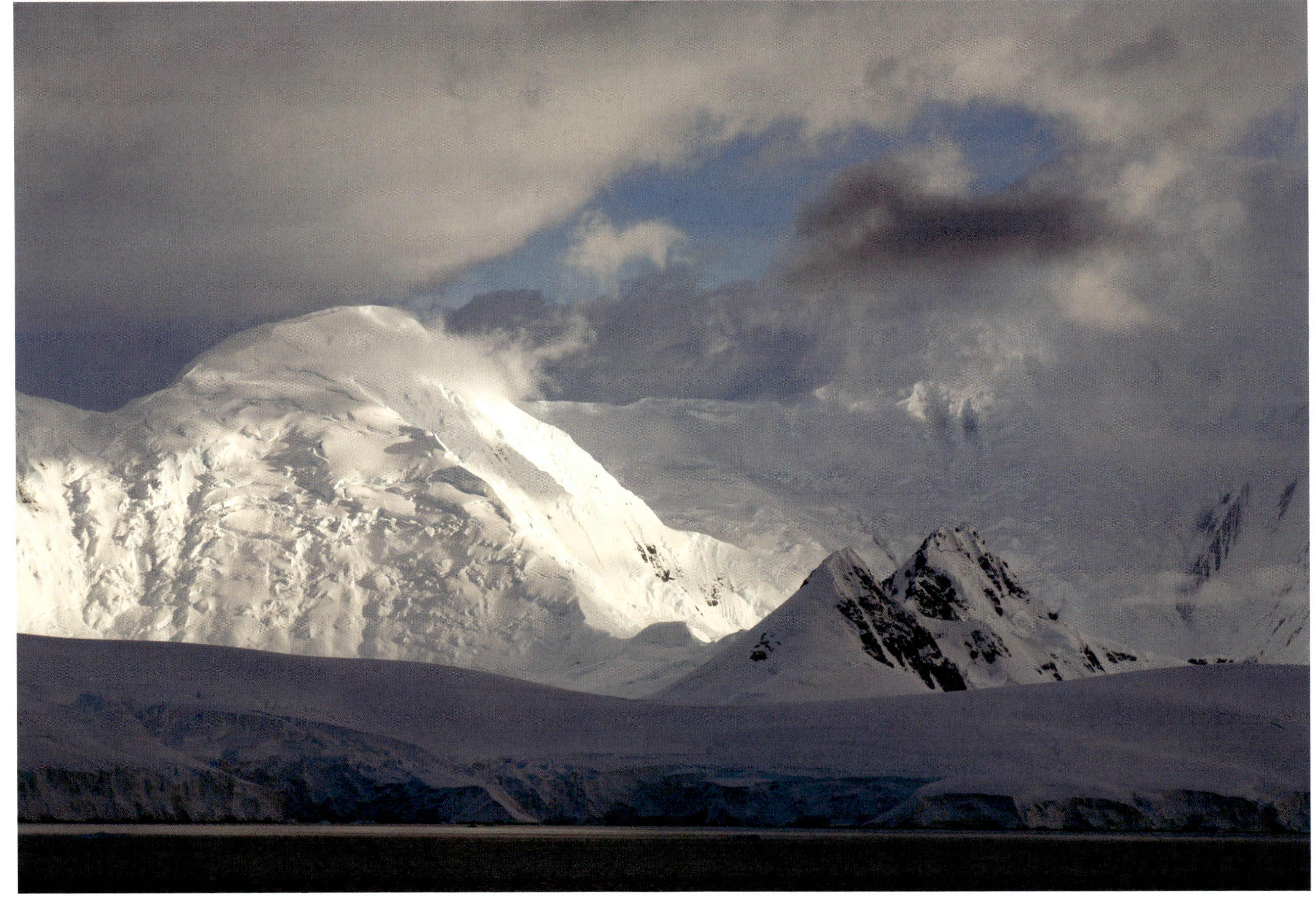

51. Landscape Panorama, Gerlache Strait, Antarctic Peninsula

The spectacular beauty of a panorama of ice-clad peaks on the coast of the Antarctic Peninsula is accentuated by a beam of sunlight. The topography here is shaped by the processes of glacial erosion and freeze-thaw. The bottom layer of glacial ice is often frozen to the solid rock underneath. As the main body of ice moves progressively downslope it tears away portions of the rock it is adhering to. In addition, when water that has seeped into cracks in the rock freezes it expands by around 9% of its volume. The ice thus formed acts like a wedge, which as a continuous cycle over time shatters the rock into angular fragments. Combined these processes create serrated peaks.

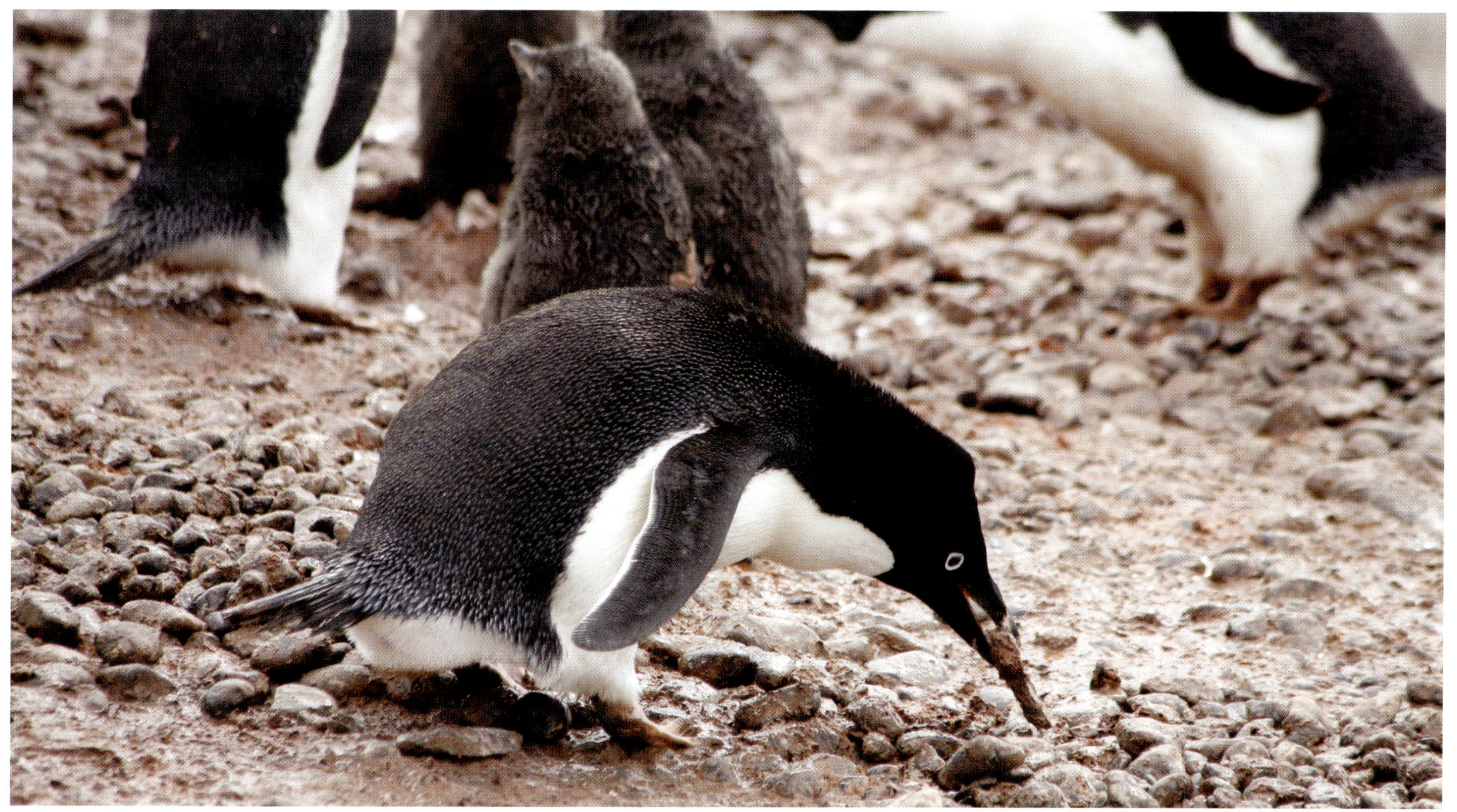

52. Adélie Penguin, Brown Bluff, Antarctic Peninsula

A young adult male Adélie penguin has picked up a small pebble which will be proffered to a potential partner as part of a mating ritual. If accepted, a platform will be made from additional pebbles which will act as a rudimentary nest. Adélies have a very dense covering of feathers, around 100 per inch, and a layer of subcutaneous fat which help to insulate the birds from cold. They feed almost exclusively on small shrimp-like crustaceans called krill. The black and white plumage pattern is termed counter-shading and helps to camouflage the birds when they are in the water.

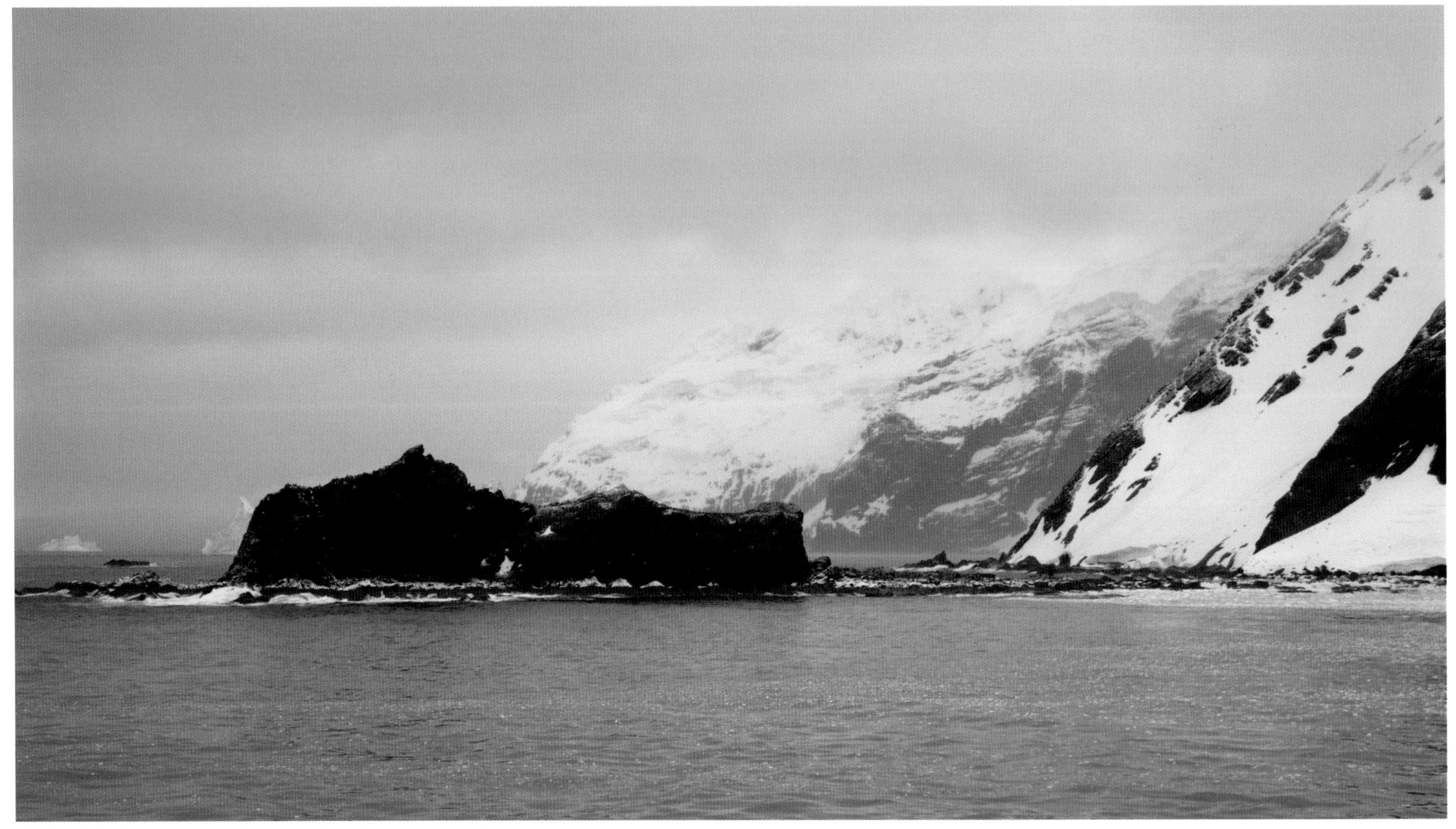

53. Point Wild, Elephant Island, Antarctica

Elephant Island is a remote rocky bastion in the infamous Drake Passage in the South Atlantic. Here at Point Wild, 22 of the crew of the *Endurance*, the ship commanded by Sir Earnest Shackleton on his ill-fated Imperial Trans-Antarctic Expedition, survived for months living beneath upturned lifeboats. Beset for 10 months in the ice, the *Endurance* had been crushed and sank in November 1915, marooning its crew of 28 men thousands of miles from help. Carried on ice floes for 5 months, they spotted the snowy peaks of Elephant Island and made a dash for it in their lifeboats. From here Shackleton and a hand-picked team sailed 800 miles across the worst seas in the world in a lifeboat to South Georgia and raised the alarm. He rescued his men on 30 August 1916 on a ship called *Yelcho* that had been borrowed from the Chilean authorities.

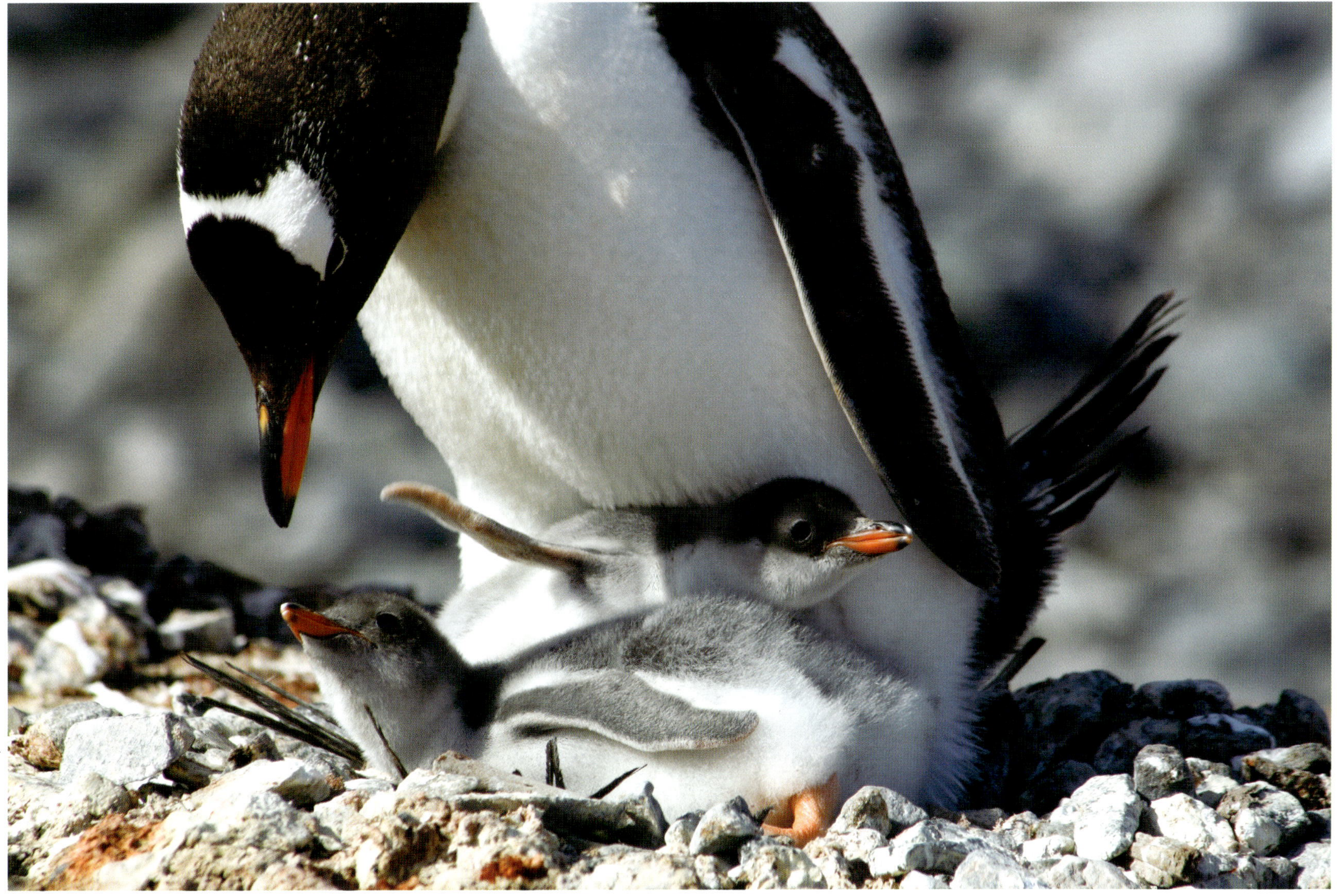

54. GENTOO PENGUIN WITH CHICKS, JOUGLA POINT, ANTARCTIC PENINSULA

A gentoo penguin carefully watches over her two chicks on a nest of small pebbles. Instinct alerts her to the incessant danger posed by skuas. These opportunistic birds are powerful and often employ a snatch-and-grab technique in pilfering chicks who innocently ramble from the safety of their nest. The breeding season for gentoos is from December to March and two eggs are laid. Incubation is shared between both parents. They feed on small fish, squid and krill. Adults grow to around 30 inches, weigh 12 pounds and have a lifespan of between 15 and 20 years. They are hunted by both leopard seals and killer whales.

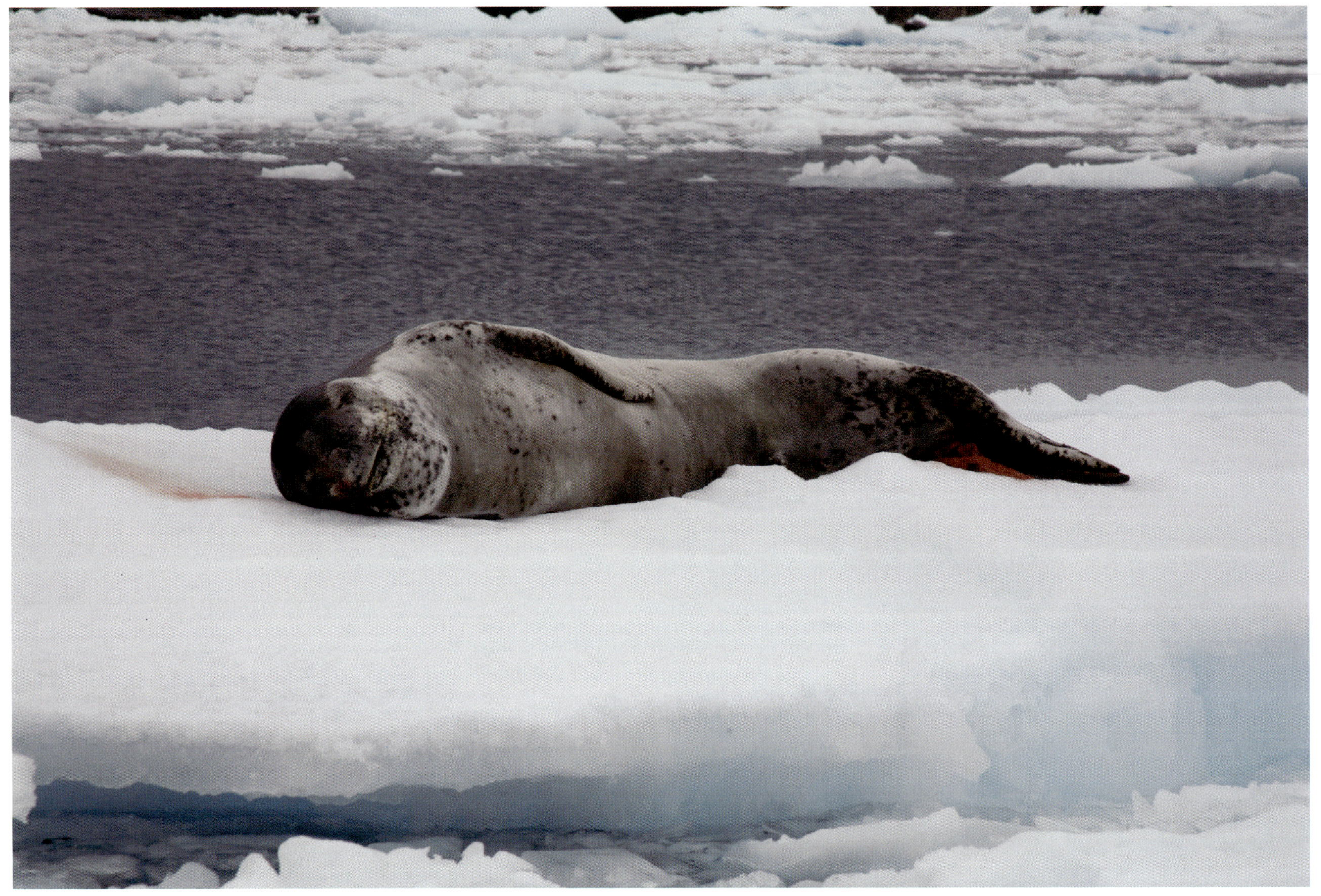

55. Leopard Seal, Cierva Cove, Antarctic Peninsula

A leopard seal dozes on an ice floe in Cierva Cove. The spots on the skin give this seal its name. They are adept at swimming and can move with impressive speed in the water. A skilled predator, their diet includes penguins, young seals, fish, squid and krill, the latter making up as much as 50% of its diet. Almost reptilian in appearance they have long sinuous bodies, large heads and an enormous mouth equipped with formidable teeth. As Adélie penguins make their way across the frozen sea to their breeding colonies on land, hunting leopard seals shadowing them can suddenly burst up through the ice and snatch a victim. They will also cruise below the surface just off-shore or along ice margins looking for prey.

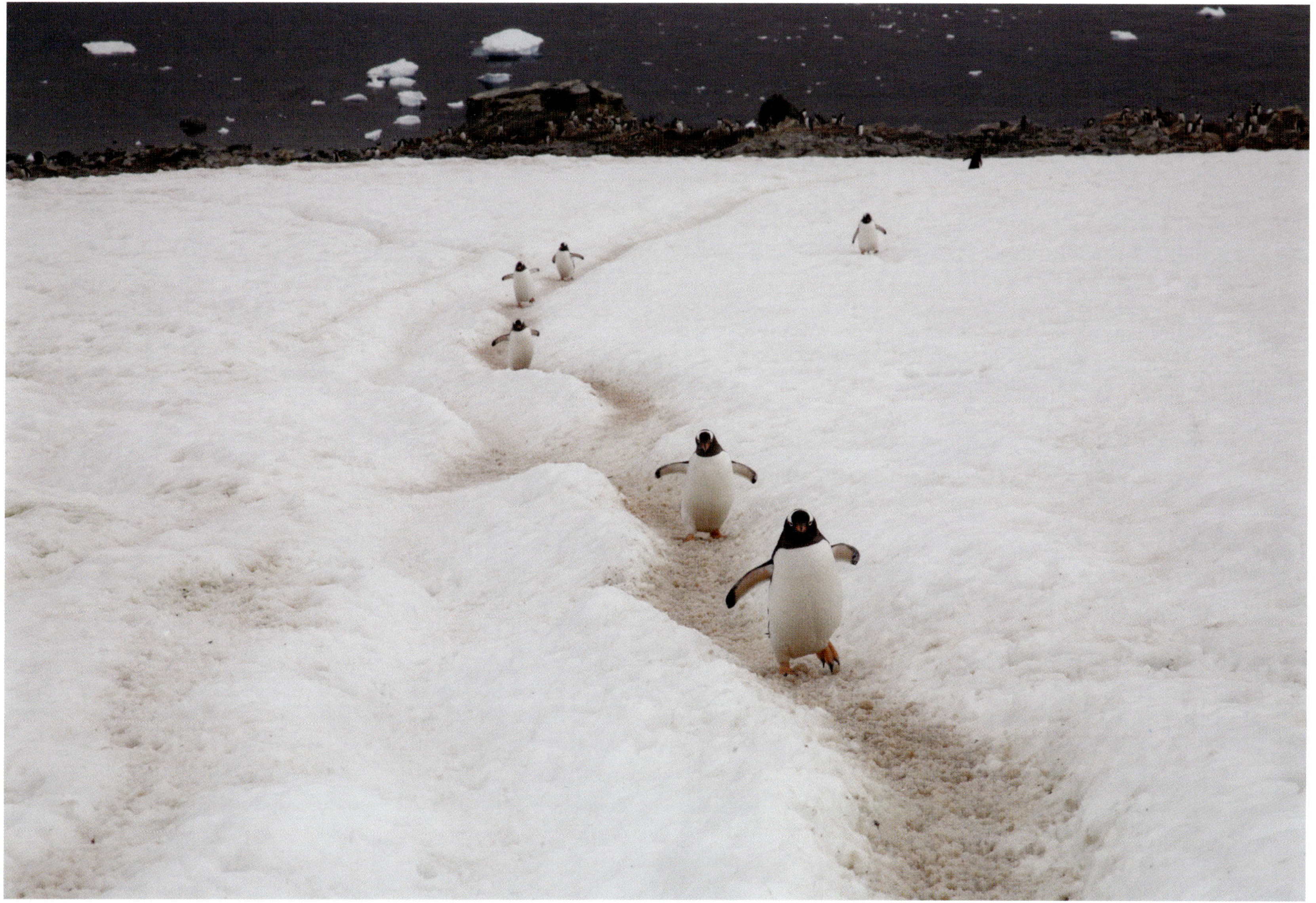

56. GENTOO PENGUINS, DANCO ISLAND, ANTARCTIC PENINSULA

There is a large colony of Gentoo penguins on Danco Island. At the height of the breeding season the adults busily trudge from the shore, their gullets laded with krill and fish to feed to their fast growing chicks. Tracks leading to the nests, which are located on the slopes several hundred feet above, are worn in the snow and ice by the constant toing and froing. Gentoo penguins have no fear of humans and will calmly pass within a couple of feet of an observer, frequently going so far as to pose for a photograph.

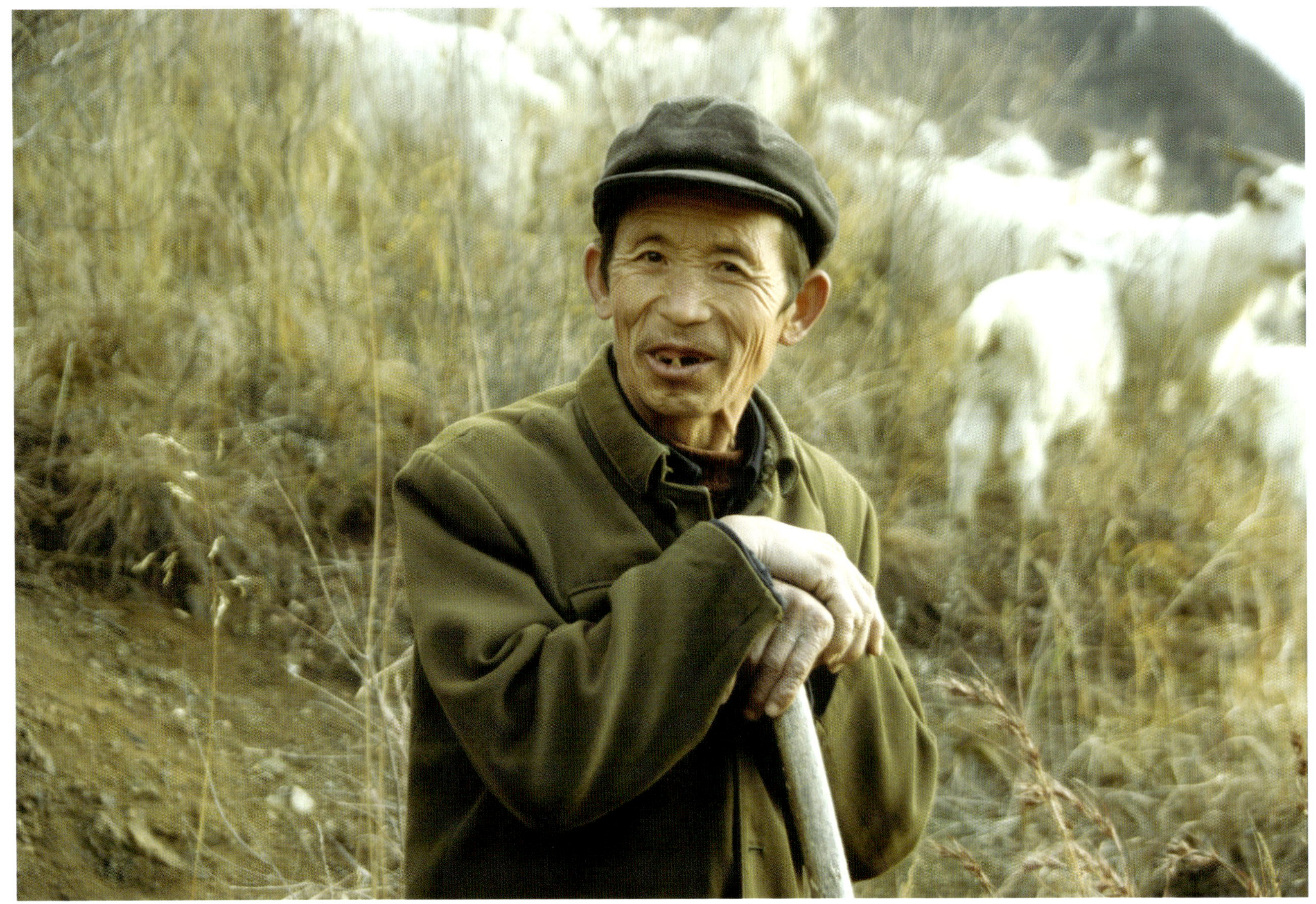

57. GOAT HERDER, XINCHEN, CHINA

Enjoying the warm October light, a goat herder poses for a photograph at a high mountain pass near his home in Xinchen. As generations of his family have done before, he tends to his small flock that he brings each day to the uplands to graze. He gently calls to the goats as he continues on his daily round, mustering and coaxing from behind. He milks them by hand back at his farmhouse in the village and at night the treasured goats are secured in a pen closeby.

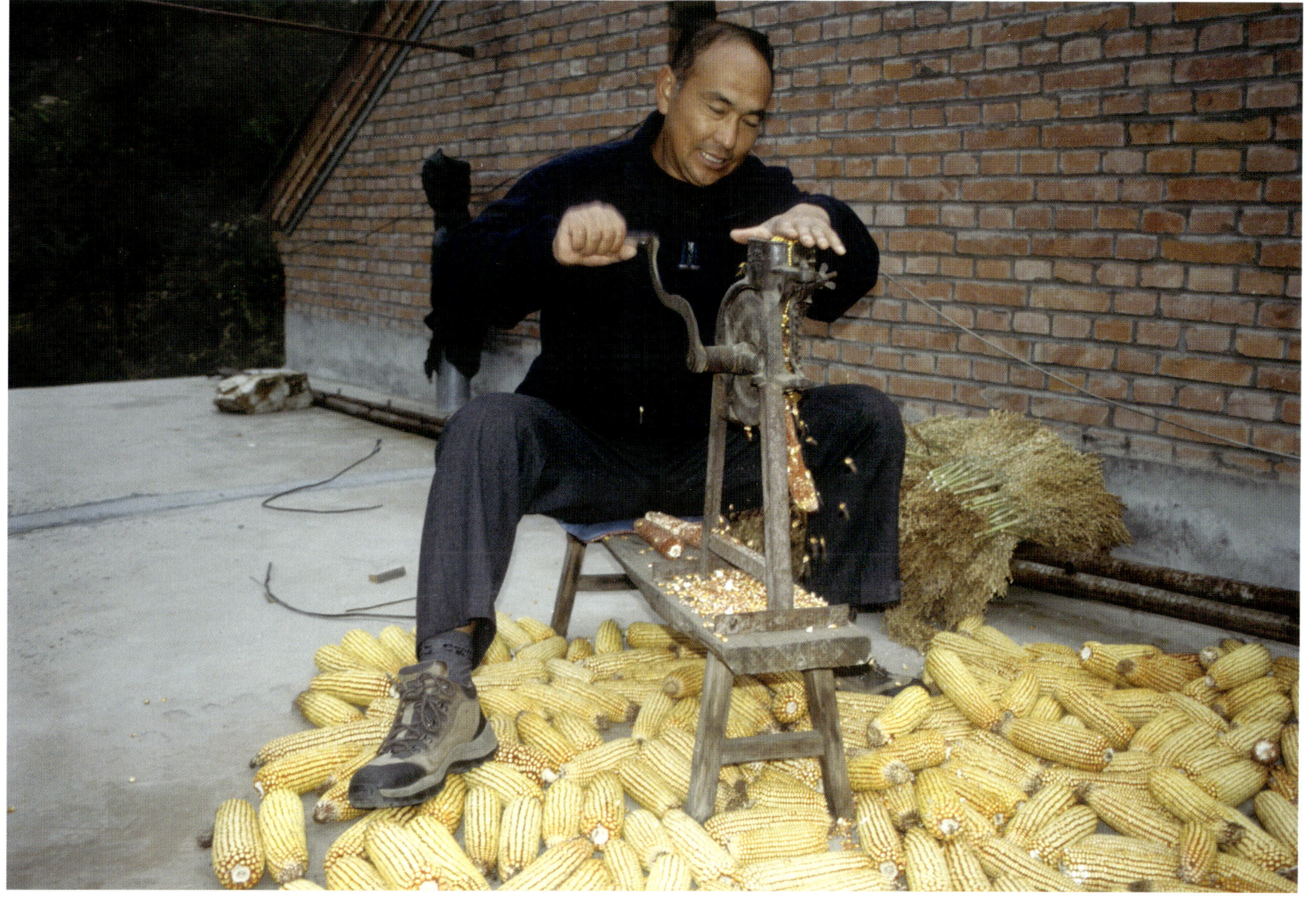

58. PROCESSING MAIZE, HUA LOU GOU, CHINA

Sitting astride his well-used hand grinder, Lao removes the kernels from a head of maize. He farms a small holding and supplements his income working as a local guide for groups of tourists visiting the Great Wall. He harvests the maize with his wife, son and daughter-in-law in September and October. All work is done by hand. The crop is brought back to his house where he processes it as the need arises. China is the largest producer of maize, the bulk of which is used for animal feed.

59. Inquisitive pig, Ganfang, China

The pig is ubiquitous in rural China. Here a youngster pokes its nose inside a rural home in search of morsels. Households usually keep several pigs which are fed primarily on corn and leftovers from the kitchen. The corn is stored outside in the yards in multi-shelved 'safes' after being brought home from the nearby fields. Prolific breeders, they are a ready source of meat. Once matured and sufficiently fattened they are usually brought to the local butcher who for a small fee dispatches and prepares them.

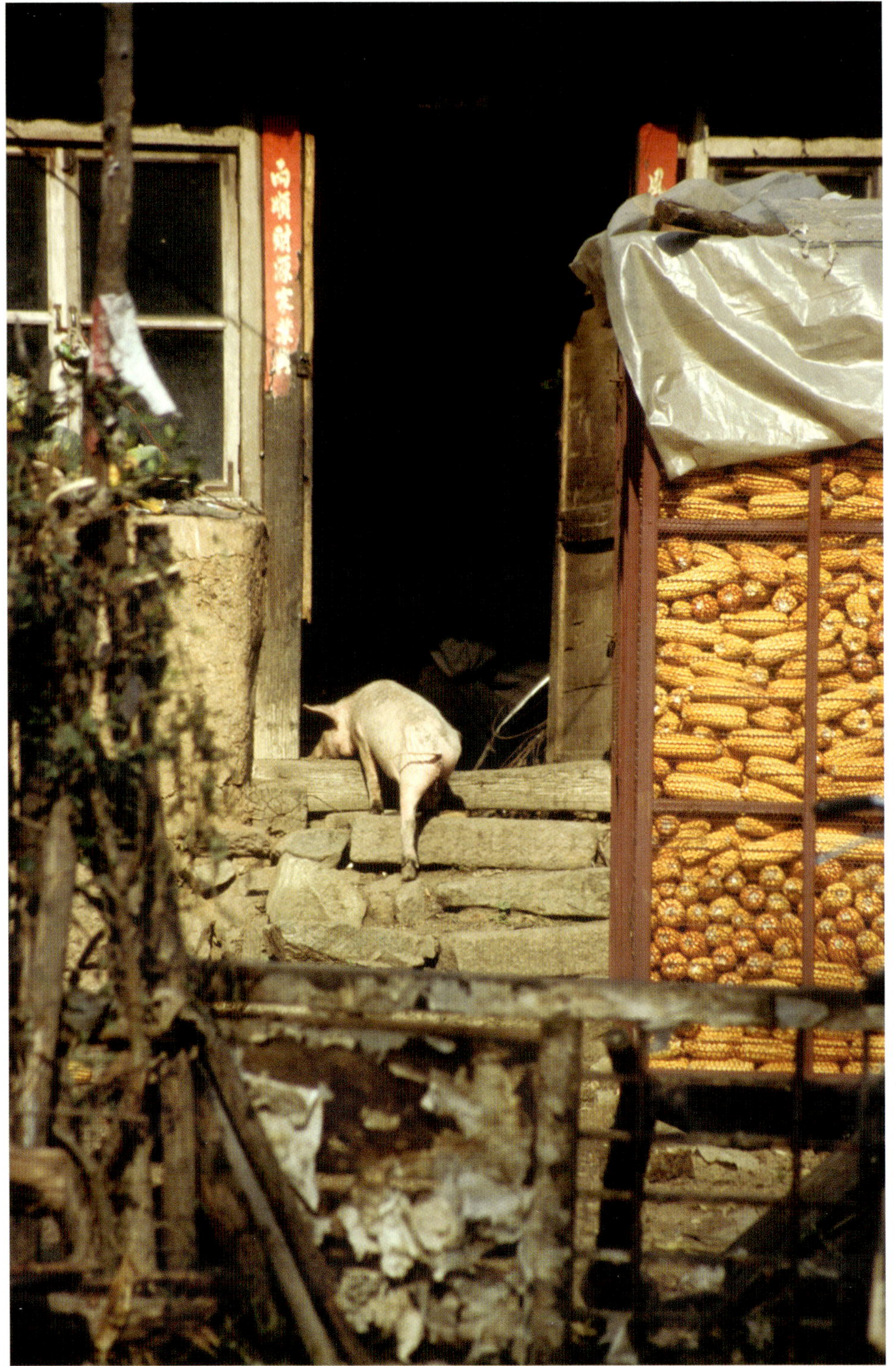

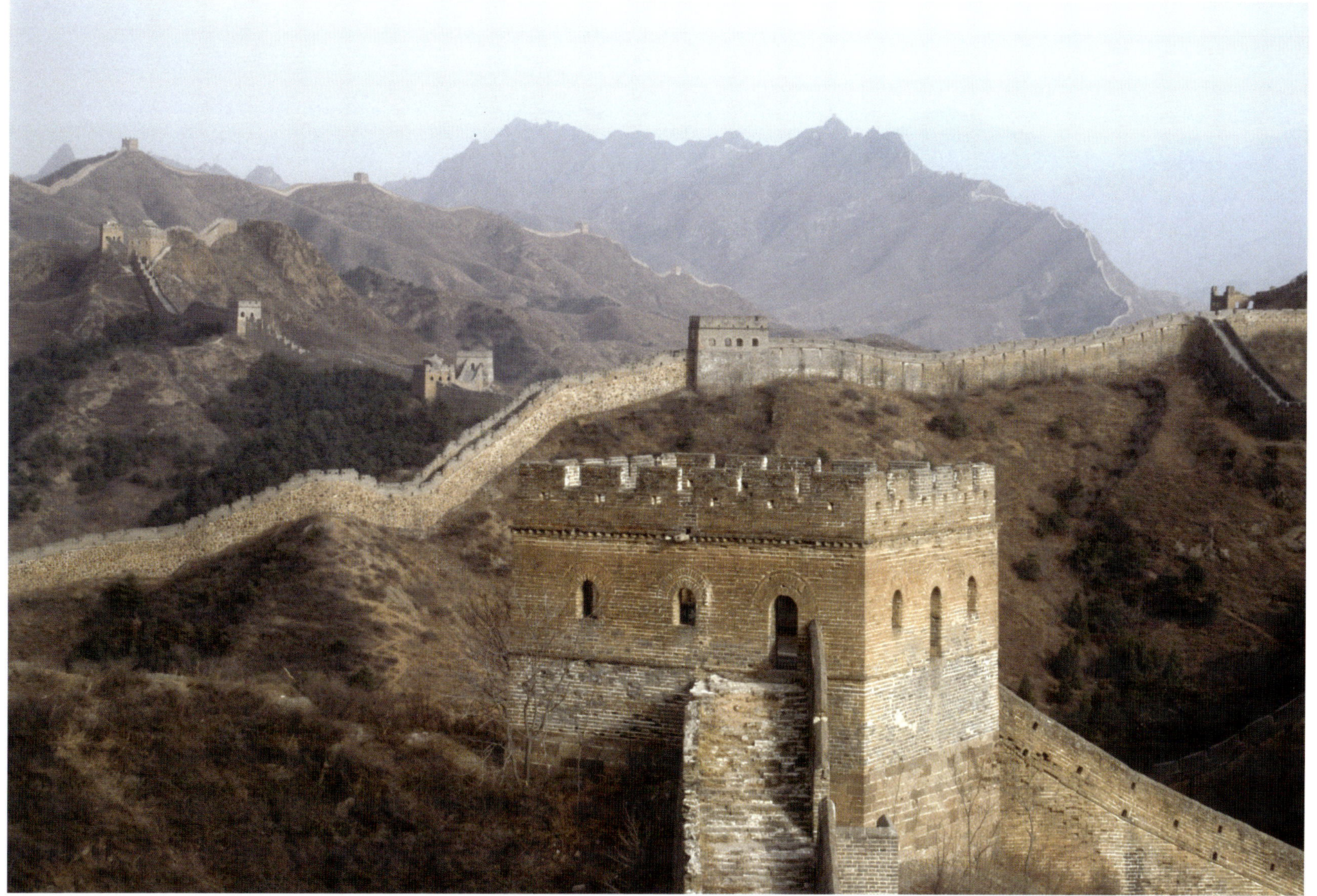

60. THE GREAT WALL, JINSHANLING, CHINA

Seemingly defying gravity the Great Wall winds its way across the undulating terrain in Jinshanling. This section was built during the Ming Dynasty and is punctuated along its length by regularly placed towers which once housed sentinels. Fires could be lit in braziers placed atop subsidiary signal towers to warn of danger. The Great Wall was built as a defensive barrier to protect China from sporadic raids by Mongol, Manchu and Tartar nomadic tribes living on the northern steppes. Spanning several dynasties it took over 2,000 years to build with the labour of millions of workers. Roughly the width of an Irish regional road, the Great Wall of China cannot be seen with the naked eye from outer space.

POSTSCRIPT

My Mother gifted me a copy of *'The Story of our Rocks and Minerals'*, a Ladybird book, for my fledgling library when I was ten years old. I was fascinated by the section on fossils. She had opened up a window on another world for me. In retrospect, this is actually where it all started. Later that same week another of those life-changing incidents was to occur. To be precise, it happened on Friday 15th August 1969 at around 8.30 pm. I remember the details vividly. My older brother Paddy was due to start that coming September at Coláiste Caoimhín, a secondary school on Parnell Road in Dublin run by the Christian Brothers.The principal, Br. Kelly, had asked for help with gardening chores around the newly built complex.

Paddy volunteered our services and that evening, with me on the bar of his pushbike, we sped like a pair of desperados up along the canal road in Harold's Cross to the school.

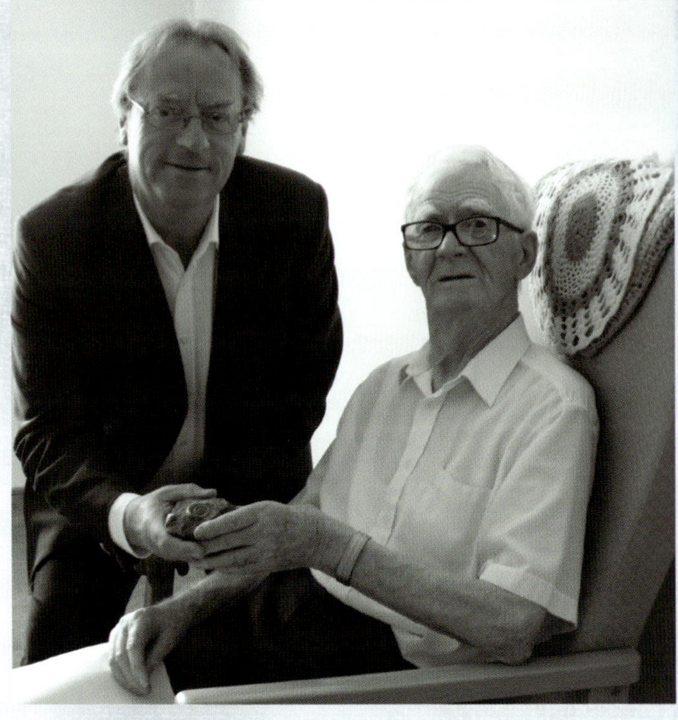

Reunited recently after 49 years - Vincent, Br. Kelly and the fossil.

Orders received, the work began. Just by pure chance I happened to be working close by Br. Kelly who was raking stones from a patch of soil that would later be sown with grass seed. He flicked a cobble over to me. 'You might find that interesting, Vincent. It's called a fossil'. I had only that week read about them in my Ladybird book.

I was enthralled as I examined the ancient shell embedded in the fragment of limestone. As a skilled teacher he instinctively recognised my genuine interest and told me that I could hang onto it. It was my first fossil. It still bears the original, handwritten label I affixed to it at home later that night and remains the most precious item in my collection.

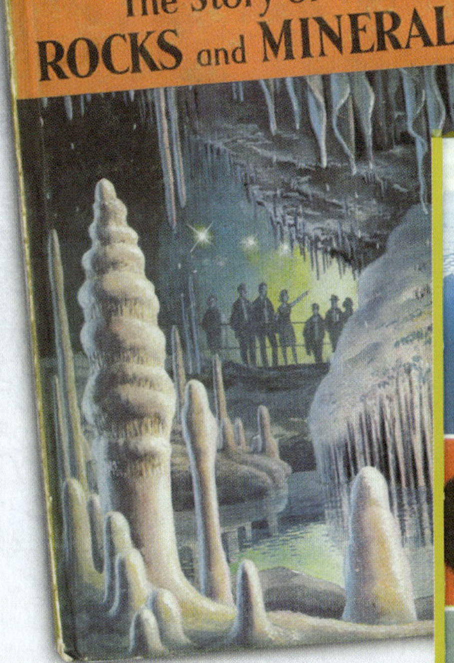

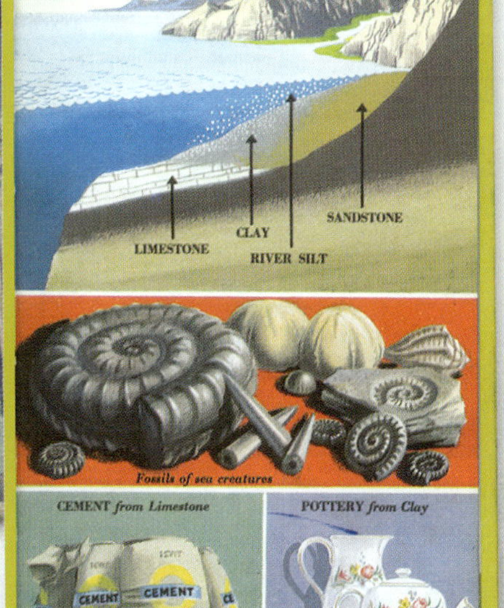

Left: My treasured Ladybird book.

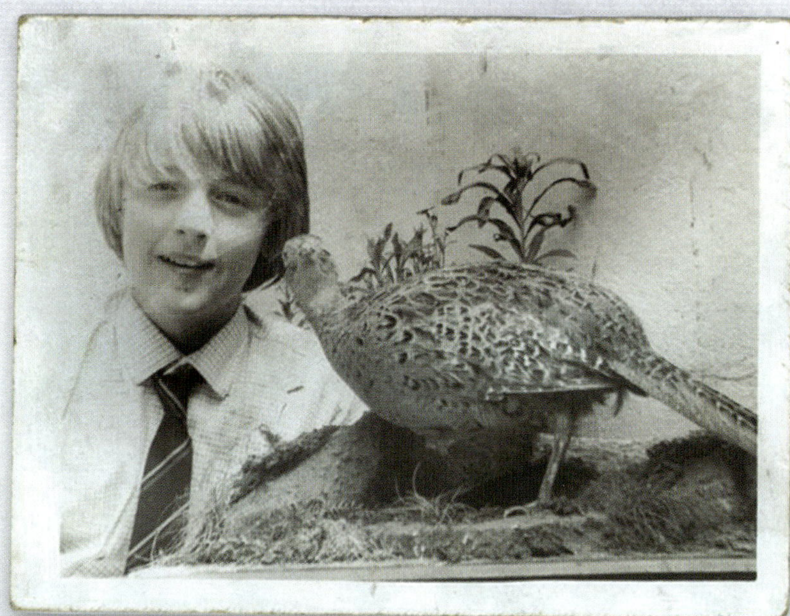

Vincent aged 10 with his stuffed pheasant 'Zulu.'

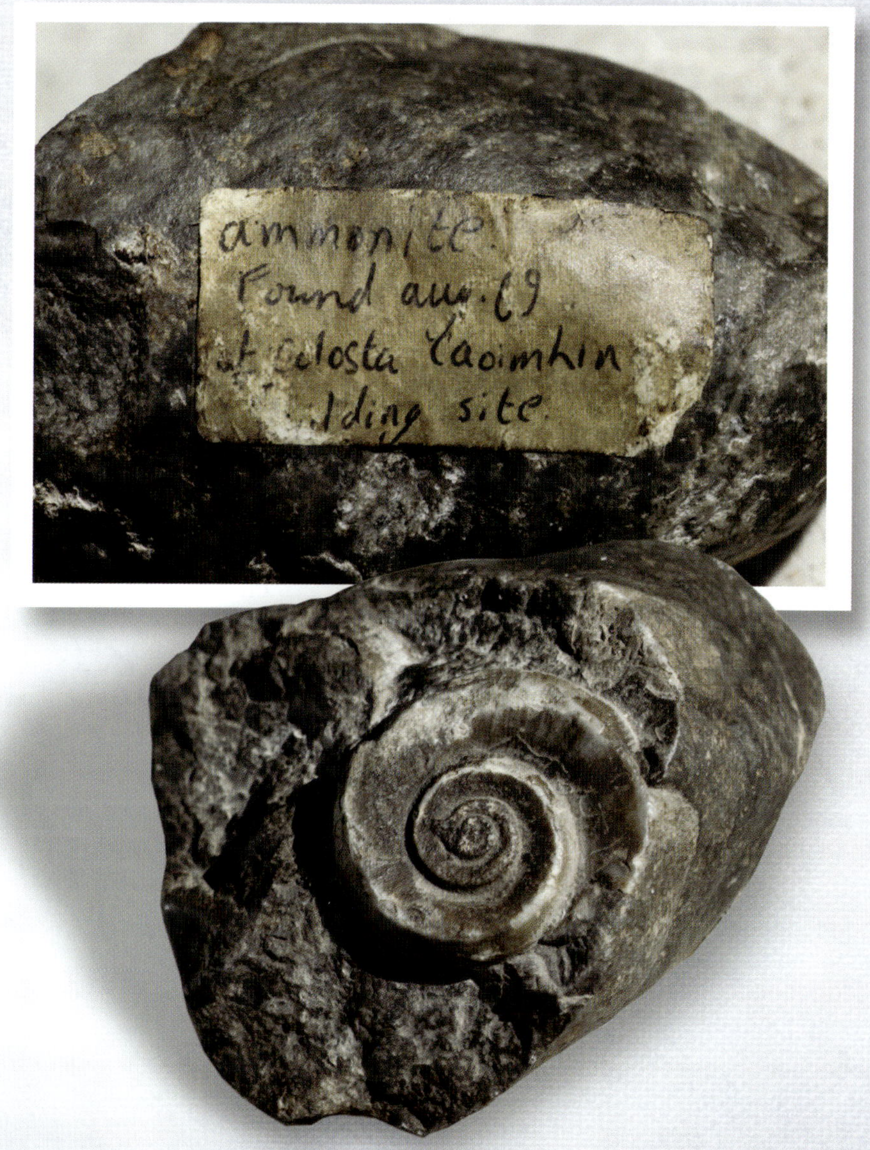

Fossil given to me by Br. Kelly found when gardening at Coláiste Caoimhín Secondary School on Parnell Road, Dublin.

Almost to the day some forty-five years later, I was standing beside three graves on a flat gravel terrace on desolate Beechey Island high in the Canadian Arctic. I had just finished explaining about the ill-fated mid-19th century Franklin Expedition to the last group of guests to come ashore. They had begun to make their way towards our landing point to be taken back to our expedition cruise ship, the *National Geographic Explorer,* anchored a short distance offshore. It had begun to snow.

As I readied to leave something on the ground caught my eye. I stooped down and picked up a piece of rock. Embedded on its surface was a delicate, fossil coral. As I examined it, the memory of a nurturing teacher leaning on his well-used rake on a sunny Friday evening many years ago came to my mind. It had indeed all come full circle.

Thank you so much Br. Kelly.

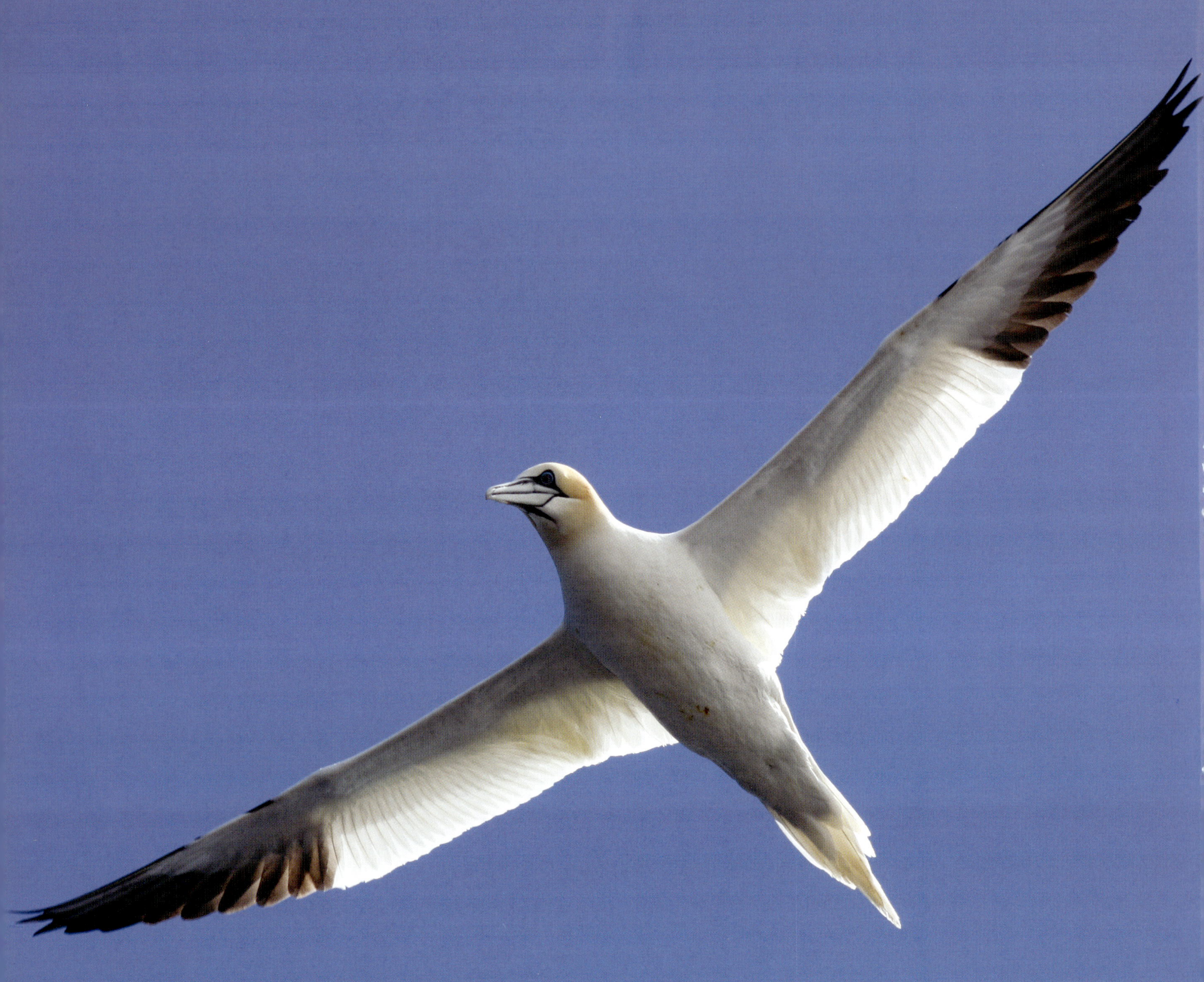

Gannet, off St. Kilda, Outer Hebrides, Scotland.

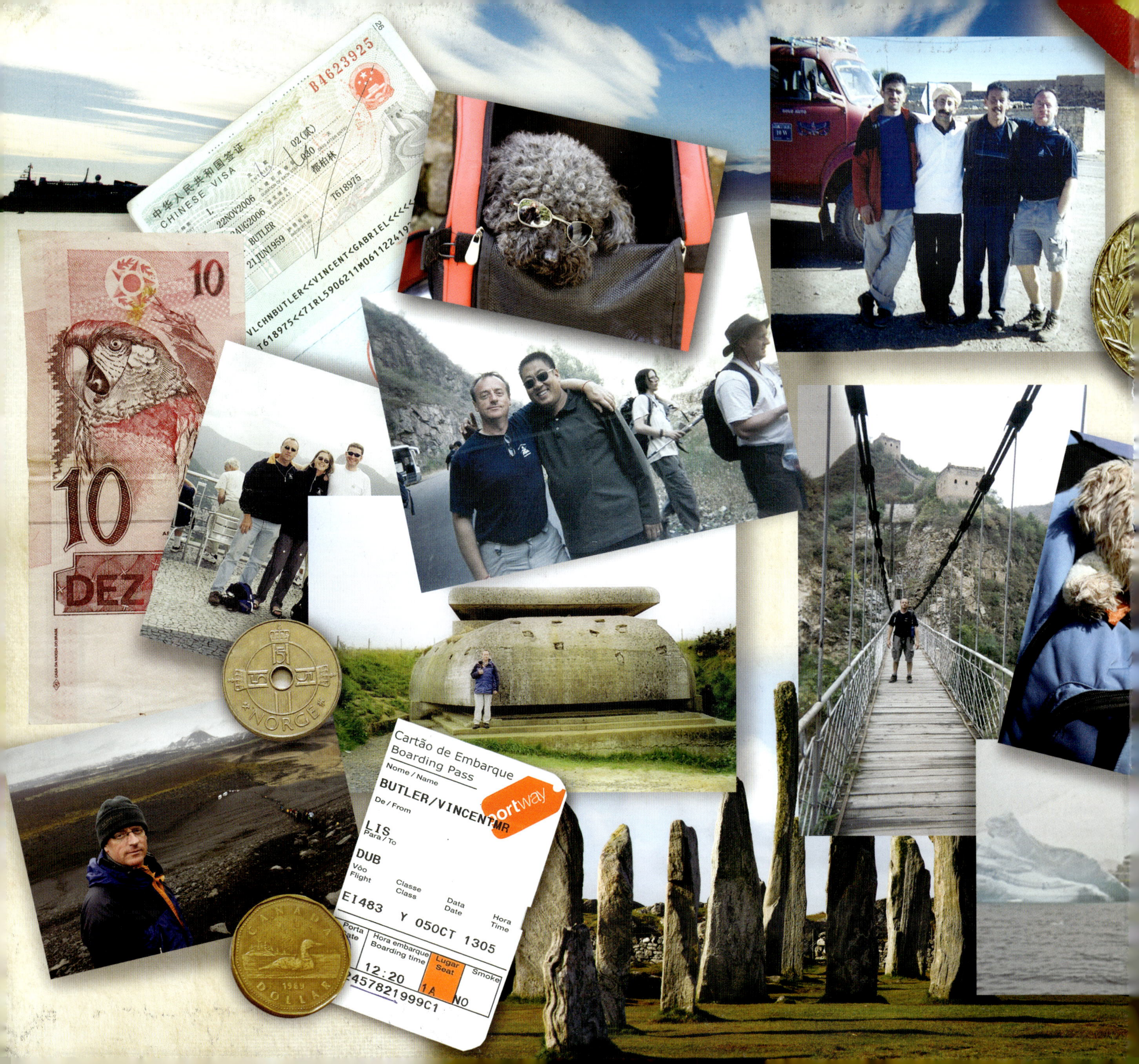

中华人民共和国签证
CHINESE VISA
B4623925
22NOV2006
BUTLER
21JUN1959
T618975
VLCHNBUTLER<<VINCENT<GABRIEL<<<<
10
10
DEZ
NORGE
CANADA
1989
DOLLAR
Cartão de Embarque
Boarding Pass
Nome / Name
BUTLER/VINCENTMR
De / From
LIS
Para / To
DUB
Vôo
Flight
Classe
Class
Data
Date
Hora
Time
EI483 Y 05OCT 1305
Porta
Gate
Hora embarque
Boarding time
Lugar
Seat
Smoke
12:20
1A
NO
2457821999C1